MILESTONES
IN MODERN
WORLD HISTORY

1600 · · · 1750 · ·   · · · 1940 · · · 2000

The
Algerian War

HEATHER LEHR WAGNER

CHELSEA HOUSE
An Infobase Learning Company

The Algerian War

Chelsea House
An imprint of Infobase Learning
132 West 31st Street
New York, NY 10001

Library of Congress Cataloging-in-Publication Data

Wagner, Heather Lehr.
The Algerian war / by Heather Lehr Wagner.
  p. cm. — (Milestones in modern world history)
Includes bibliographical references and index.
ISBN 978-1-60413-923-5 (hardcover)
1. Algeria—History—Revolution, 1954–1962—Juvenile literature. 2. National liberation movements—Algeria—Juvenile literature. 3. France—Colonies—Africa—History—Juvenile literature. I. Title. II. Series: Milestones in modern world history.
DT295.W25 2012
965'.046--dc23   2011023060

Chelsea House books are available at special discounts when purchased in bulk quantities for businesses, associations, institutions, or sales promotions. Please call our Special Sales Department in New York at (212) 967-8800 or (800) 322-8755.

You can find Chelsea House on the World Wide Web at http://www.infobaselearning.com.

Text design by Erik Lindstrom
Cover design by Alicia Post
Composition by Keith Trego
Cover printed by Yurchak Printing, Landisville, Pa.
Book printed and bound by Yurchak Printing, Landisville, Pa.
Date printed: January 2012
Printed in the United States of America

10 9 8 7 6 5 4 3 2 1

CONTENTS

One War Ends, Another Begins

May 8, 1945, was a day of glorious celebration in France. Having spent five years under Nazi control, France was now joining the world in celebrating the defeat of Adolf Hitler's Germany and the end of fighting in Europe. World War II was drawing to a close.

In Paris, French women danced with the victorious British and American soldiers, whose presence in the capital demonstrated the end of the war in Europe. The Arc de Triomphe was illuminated. Once again, lights shone on the Trocadero fountains and the Place de la Concorde. Throngs of people, cheering and celebrating, filled the streets. There was enormous relief in France—relief that the war was ending (and would be completely over with the defeat of Nazi Germany's ally, Japan, in August 1945), that bombings and battles would no longer mark

French citizens march in victory down the Champs-Élysées, in Paris, on May 8, 1945—also known as Victory in Europe Day. At the same time the French were celebrating their freedom from Nazi oppression, many in the French colony of Algeria were longing to be freed from French rule.

daily life, that the shortages and miseries that occupation had brought to the nation might finally be at an end.

On that same day, in a different French territory, the streets of a town filled with people who also spoke of liberation. But for the people of Sétif, in the French colony of Algeria in North Africa, their liberation had not yet come. They, too, wanted to be freed from what they viewed as an occupying power. But for these Algerians, the liberation they were seeking was from France.

News of the liberation of Europe from the German threat had brought mixed emotions in Algeria. Algeria had been a colony of France since 1830, when French troops landed at a beach 20 miles (32 kilometers) west of the capital city of Algiers. Years of fighting followed until finally, in 1847, Algeria was declared to be part of France. Its lands were later divided into three French administrative regions, or departments.

AN ENDURING PEACE

Everett McKinley Dirksen traveled through Europe in 1945 as a representative of the U.S. House Committee on Appropriations. He inspected American embassies, reconstruction agencies, and the armed forces. On May 8, 1945, he was in Paris when news of the end of the war in Europe filled the streets, sparking joyful celebrations. Dirksen recorded his thoughts in a letter excerpted below:

> People, young and old, have been seeking to cast off restraint. . . . Planes zoomed over the Arc de Triomphe. Flags are everywhere. Youngsters are parading. The bells proclaimed the glad fact of an armistice. . . . The spirit of victory was in the air; it was everywhere—in hearts, and minds and faces of people. It was over, in part, a load had been lifted. . . .
> Will we succeed this time in building a structure of peace that shall have full and fair opportunity to endure? I wonder. I've seen some things . . . that are disturbing. Already I see Freedom being mocked and leached away in certain places. . . . I see the selfish grasping for power, the economic advantage which can only weaken and then destroy that sense of fairness and that faith which is so requisite to a well-ordered and contented world.*

* Everett M. Dirksen Papers, May 8, 1945, Personal, f. 34, http://www.dirksencenter.org/1945trip/may8text.htm.

In the mid-nineteenth century, the French government set about colonizing Algeria with French settlers. When few French people—apart from the unemployed or those forcibly deported to the colony—expressed an interest in relocating to North Africa, France opened the doors to other European settlers, many of them from Spain, Malta, and Corsica. These colonists from France and other parts of Europe, known as *colons*, were given Algerian land. The French government, as early as 1844, declared the right to seize any "undeveloped land" unless an Algerian could show a legal document proving his right to it.[1] By the end of the nineteenth century, when the flow of European immigrants to Algeria began to slow, any remaining large parcels of unclaimed land were given to private investment companies to farm or use as they saw fit.

Gradually, Algeria became populated by two separate communities—the original inhabitants of the North African lands, many of them Muslim, and the European settlers and their descendants. The large cities and the best lands were in the hands of the colons, even though they formed a minority of the population. The two groups lived essentially separate lives in a segregated society. Algeria was governed as if it were part of France, but the native Algerians were not considered French citizens, nor were they admitted to French schools or allowed the same political representation as, for example, a resident of Paris or Lyon.

In the 1930s, a centennial festival was organized to celebrate the hundredth anniversary of Algeria becoming part of France. Several political movements were organized in Algeria around this time to ensure greater rights for Algerians. These relatively moderate movements had a simple aim: for Algerians to receive the rights of French citizenship. If Algeria was part of France, these moderate protesters argued, then all Algerians should receive the same rights, the same access to French schools, and the same political representation as those living in other parts of France.

The former governor-general of Algeria, a Frenchman named Maurice Viollette, wisely sensed the need for a swift and competent response to these moderate requests. He prepared a series of reforms for the French Assembly—France's equivalent of the U.S. House of Representatives. His 1936 proposal, known as the Blum-Viollette bill, offered citizenship to a small percentage of Muslims and laid the foundation for a process in which Algeria might more thoroughly be assimilated into France. His goal was that "Muslim students, while remaining Muslim, should become so French in their education, that no Frenchman, however deeply racist and religiously prejudiced he might be . . . will any longer dare to deny them French fraternity."[2]

The bill's modest aims nonetheless met fierce protest from those colons who feared that greater assimilation of native Algerians might threaten their own power and influence as a highly privileged Algerian minority. Many of the protests had racist and anti-Muslim overtones. In the wake of a growing unrest in Algeria, the bill was abandoned in 1938 without ever coming to a vote in the National Assembly. Viollette issued an insightful warning to the Assembly:

> When the Muslims protest, you are indignant; when they approve, you are suspicious; when they keep quiet you are fearful. *Messieurs*, these men have no political nation. They do not even demand their religious nation. All they ask is to be admitted into yours. If you refuse this, beware lest they do not soon create one for themselves.[3]

FIGHTING FOR FRANCE

The events of World War II would have a dramatic impact on France and its colonies. Having tried first to appease Hitler and his regime as he conquered Austria and Czechoslovakia, the leaders of France and Great Britain were forced to recognize Hitler's determination to conquer much of Europe when Nazi troops invaded Poland on September 1, 1939. Shortly thereafter, France and Britain declared war on Germany. By 1940, German troops had conquered the Netherlands, Luxembourg, and Belgium. They then turned toward France, sweeping through the Ardennes on May 13. Within six weeks, France—one of the most powerful nations in Europe—was defeated.

In short order, German troops occupied much of northern France. The southern zone, as well as the French territories in North Africa, were marginally under the control of the Vichy government—the French political administration that the Nazis permitted to govern the portions of France that were not occupied by German troops. The Vichy government could only pass laws that did not interfere with German laws. Vichy officials collaborated with the occupying forces in many ways, most clearly in aiding in the roundup of Jews and other French citizens deemed "undesirable" by the Nazis.

France's quick defeat at the hands of Germany, and the weakened and largely ineffective Vichy government that was put in place in France by the Nazis, made a deep impression in Algeria. A defeated France was no longer a mighty colonial power that could dictate terms to Algerians. The wartime shortages further cemented the injustice of segregated life in Algeria. Muslims suffered more from the economic hardships and shortages of food and heating oil than others. Starving children rooted through trashcans, desperate for a few scraps of food.

At the same time, Algerians provided many troops who fought bravely for the Allied cause, supporting the country that still refused to honor them with citizenship. Fighting alongside British and American soldiers, many of these Algerians gradually became exposed to the kinds of freedoms and privileges that they did not enjoy at home. In Algeria, the Vichy government banned all Algerian political parties. Political leaders were imprisoned. The majority of food supplies were shipped off to Germany. Ration cards determined who received food and how much. In Algeria, there were different-colored ration cards for "Europeans" and "natives." Those holding the "European" ration cards received more and higher quality food from better-stocked distribution centers.[4]

After Germany had finally been defeated, the Algerians were left to wonder about their status. They had helped to liberate the country that refused to liberate them. Now, as France celebrated its freedom, many in Algeria wondered how they could celebrate a return to an occupation by the very country for which they had fought.

THE FIRST SHOTS

On May 8, 1945, a celebration was organized in the town of Sétif in northeastern Algeria to mark the end of the war in Europe. In Sétif, home to a large Muslim population, there were rumblings of discontent from a growing number of Algerian protesters who sought independence from France. The town had suffered greatly from food shortages during the war, and a drought that had lasted nearly five months added to the shortages.

The mayor of Sétif learned that a demonstration was being organized in support of Algerian independence, timed to coincide with the May 8 celebrations. But he had just 20 policemen at his disposal—hardly enough officers to block a large demonstration. He also had little desire to halt the planned celebration. Instead, he issued an order that no demonstrations could have any kind of a political theme, nor could there be any banners or signs that urged independence.

When the first banners were unfurled, proclaiming an "Independent Algeria," the police moved in to seize the offending signs. Shots were fired. It remains unclear who fired first or why, but the small police force was quickly overwhelmed and forced to retreat. Armed protesters then spread out through the town and into the countryside, targeting the colons and any symbols of French administration. Altogether, about 100 Europeans were murdered over five days of looting and violence, and another hundred were wounded.[5]

Finally, French authorities were able to assemble some troops and transport them to Algeria. A fierce retaliation began. Villages with large Muslim populations were subjected to summary executions, bombings, and other brutalities. Vigilante groups were formed and armed; many of them simply seized Muslims and butchered them.

French reports ultimately estimated the number of Muslim dead in this misguided effort at reestablishing the peace in Algeria to be between 1,020 and 1,300. Radio stations in Cairo, Egypt, broadcast a figure of 45,000. The exact figure can never be known, but most historians agree that at least 6,000 Muslims were slaughtered to avenge the death of 100 Europeans.[6]

Few people in France learned of the events at Sétif or of their army's role in suppressing Algerian protests. The country was busy celebrating freedom and liberation in Europe. But in Algeria, the brutality of French forces underlined the message that Algerians would never truly be considered French citizens nor would they enjoy the kind of freedom that the rest of France was now welcoming—at least not without fighting for it. Algerian soldiers, who were returning from fighting for France in the war, were horrified to learn of the murder of so many of their people at the hands of French soldiers.

The Algerian war for independence would not officially begin for another nine and a half years. But many historians believe its first shots were fired in Sétif in May 1945, while the rest of France celebrated Europe's freedom.

North African Conquest

The struggle for independence marked Algerian life for centuries. The country's location and size made it a key target for those who long wanted to seize a large chunk of North Africa.

Algeria is located in the center of Africa's northern coast, across the Mediterranean Sea from Spain and France. It occupies more than 2.38 million square kilometers of land (approximately 900,000 square miles), making it the tenth largest country in the world and the largest in Africa. It is nearly 3.5 times the size of the state of Texas. England, France, Germany, Spain, Portugal, Italy, and Poland could all fit comfortably inside Algeria's borders.

Despite its vast size, not all of Algeria is quality land. Algeria is marked by vast stretches of desert. Because the Sahara takes

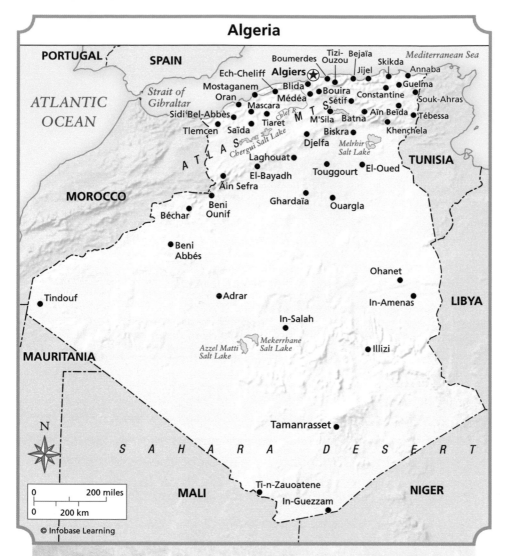

Algeria

The country today known as Algeria gained its independence from France in 1962. It had been a French colony since 1830; prior to that, various dynasties and empires had controlled it since antiquity. It is the largest country in Africa and on the Mediterranean Sea, though much of its southern territory is desert and its population is concentrated on the Mediterranean coast.

up approximately 90 percent of Algeria's land, the majority of its larger cities are clustered in the northern half of the country, closer to the Mediterranean. Less than 10 percent of Algeria's population lives in the Saharan region. While the northern border of Algeria lies along the Mediterranean, neighboring nations to the west are Morocco and Mauritania. Tunisia and Libya lie to the east, and Mali and Niger touch Algeria's southern borders.

The vastness of Algeria means that each region of the country has a unique and distinctive atmosphere. Cities in the north—including Oran, Constantine, and the capital of Algiers—are bustling and crowded. There you can find evidence of the empires that conquered Algeria, including Rome, Spain, and France. A trip along the Trans-Saharan Highway leads into oasis towns and settlements occupied by small tribes. Seemingly endless stretches of sand rise in dunes, and only occasionally are they interrupted by natural rock formations—evidence of volcanic eruptions millions of years ago.

The name Algeria came from its capital city, Algiers. Both are thought to be derived from the Arabic word *Al-Jaza'ir*, a name given to a small group of islands off the coast of Algiers that became part of the mainland in the sixteenth century. Before the sixteenth century, the specific territory we know today as Algeria did not exist. Instead, it was part of the larger region of northern Africa that fell victim to a succession of conquering empires.

THOSE WHO CAME

Legend suggests that among those who chose to settle in Algeria were 20 companions of the Greek hero Heracles (in Roman myth, Hercules), who sailed into the bay at Algiers, fell in love with its hills and rich farmland, and never left. It can be difficult to separate fact from fiction in the rich and colorful history of those who have moved in and out of Algeria. However, it is clear that its position on the Mediterranean has made it an important gateway into Africa for a succession of peoples.

This history begins in the Sahara, which—hundreds of millions of years ago—was not desert but sea. Scientific studies and excavations have shown that these seas gradually, tens of millions of years ago, transformed into desert—a desert larger than the Sahara of today. Then, around 10,500 years ago, a sudden burst of monsoon rains over this enormous desert transformed much of the region into habitable land. Lakes and forests dotted the Sahara, while to the north Europe was covered by uninhabitable sheets of ice as a result of the last ice age.

It was during this time that two groups moved into the region: the Oranian and the Capsian. While some indigenous people lived in the region—generally nomadic tribes that moved across portions of North Africa—the Oranian and Capsian were the first to introduce farming techniques to the region. When their farming proved beneficial, they became the first permanent settlements in Algeria. Rock paintings and carvings made at that time still exist, including in Algeria's Tassili N'Ajjer National Park, displaying what life was like for these earliest settlers.

The Berbers descended from these settlers. Naming the different groups that have constituted Algeria's population throughout its history can be tricky, as names used by one group to refer to another may not be used by the group itself. Only recently have the Berbers begun to refer to themselves by that name, but the word has long been used to refer to the native population that occupied the region before the various periods of conquest. Berbers speak a wide range of dialects and maintain their loyalty to their tribe. They also oppose any form of foreign or religious domination. The name is thought to come from the ancient Greeks, who used the word *barbaros* to describe *anyone* not living within what they considered to be civilization. The ancient Romans employed the Latin word *barbari* in a similar fashion.

As ancient civilizations began to master the use of ships in conquering territory, Algeria's strategic location on the Mediterranean made it a prime target. The Phoenicians were the next group to arrive in the region, around 1000 B.C. Because the Phoenicians were involved in trading raw materials from what is today known as Spain, they established several small ports along Algeria's Mediterranean coast during that time. These trading posts gradually grew into market towns, where traders slowly built relationships with the Berbers, providing them with goods to ensure their cooperation along the trade route.

Around 814 B.C., the Phoenicians established a North African capital in Carthage (in modern-day Tunis). The Carthaginians gradually gained more control over North Africa by pushing the Berbers into the mountains or into the Sahara to protect their trade routes or, alternately, by seizing the Berber men and forcing them to serve in the Carthaginian army. By the fourth century B.C., Berbers made up the largest single group in that army.

But the Roman Republic was on the rise. Decades of warfare followed as Romans and Phoenicians struggled for control of North Africa. During that period (around the second century B.C.), a series of Berber kingdoms were established in Algeria and began to grow in power. With the conquering Phoenicians weakened by battles with Rome on numerous fronts, the Berbers were able to seize control of their own lands. One of the largest of these Berber kingdoms was at Numidia, in northeastern Algeria.

After the Romans conquered Carthage, in 146 B.C., Rome began to establish control over much of North Africa. The Berber kingdoms resisted Roman conquest for several decades, but gradually they weakened. By 105 B.C., a Roman colony was established in the lands controlled by the Berbers. As was the custom, territory was given to Roman veterans of the wars that had provided Rome with the territory in the first place. Around 40 A.D., a province of what was now the Roman Empire—Mauretania Caesariensis—was established in the region. Its capital was Caesarea, in the land we know today as Algeria.

ROMAN RULE

For more than 400 years, the Roman Empire ruled Algeria, a region that played a key role in helping the empire flourish.

The ports in Algeria provided an important gateway between the demands of Roman life and the rich resources provided by its African colony. Africa was an important supplier of grain to Rome. It also supplied the gold and ivory used in the fabrication of tools, crafts, and jewelry. Slaves passed through Algerian ports on their way to Rome, as did the wild animals—including lions and tigers—that were featured in exhibitions and competitions in the Roman amphitheaters.

Gradually, Roman settlers began to build their own communities, founding the towns of Tipasa (the modern Tipaza), Cuicul (Djemila), Thamugadi (Timgad), and Sitifis (Sétif). Particularly in northern Algeria, Roman rule brought wealth and growth. Successful Berbers were able to gain Roman citizenship. Large public buildings were erected in the towns, evidence of the prosperity of those who benefited from the Roman presence.

But not all of the Berbers welcomed Roman rule. As more Romans moved into the surrounding areas to build homes and establish farms, they often seized land from those who were living there. Many of the tribes fought back. Finally, Roman Emperor Trajan, who ruled from A.D. 98 to 117, ordered the construction of a line of forts to mark the southern limits of Roman rule. Rebellions continued, increasing around the fourth century, as the Roman Empire began to weaken.

THE VANDALS ARRIVE

A weakened Rome meant opportunity for various groups desperate to seize territory, one of which was the Vandals. The Vandals were a Germanic tribe that eventually and briefly conquered portions of modern-day Spain, France, Italy, and North Africa as the Roman Empire collapsed. They plundered Rome in A.D. 455 in an attack so fierce and destructive that the word *vandal* (someone who willfully destroys property) comes from their actions in the city.

Before the Vandals sacked Rome, they launched an attack on the territory in North Africa. They were led by King

Gaiseric, who was determined to increase the wealth and power of his people. Having engaged in several fierce battles with the Visigoths for control of Spain, Gaiseric recognized an opportunity across the Mediterranean in North Africa, where the weakened Roman Empire presented far less of a challenge than the Visigoths. After overseeing the construction of a Vandal fleet, he was determined to resettle all of his people—some 80,000 of them—in North Africa. In A.D. 429, these Vandal men, women, and children boarded boats and sailed across the Mediterranean, quickly seizing much of northeastern Algeria.

One of the fiercest battles was in Hippo Regius, a city that today is known as Annaba. The bishop of Hippo Regius was Augustine, whose writings had made him one of the leading thinkers in the early Christian church. He died during the Vandal siege of Hippo Regius and would later be recognized as a saint by the Roman Catholic Church. For 14 months, the Vandals and Romans fought for control of Hippo Regius; in 432, Roman Emperor Valentinian III formally acknowledged King Gaiseric as the ruler of the North African lands he had conquered. Hippo Regius became the capital of Gaiseric's kingdom. Later, after the Vandals had conquered Carthage, their capital was moved there.

The Vandals proved adept at conquest, but they lacked the Roman talent for administering territories. For three decades, they functioned almost like pirates, roaming the Mediterranean, raiding ports, and seizing property and goods. Gradually, as the Vandals focused on ports and towns where they might obtain the most profit, small Berber tribes in the outlying areas began to band together to fight off any Vandals who might move into their region.

An attack by Emperor Justinian of Byzantium ultimately led to the defeat of the Vandals. The Byzantines seized only a few of the coastal towns, plus Timgad in the northeast. The remainder of Algeria became increasingly chaotic, as various Berber tribes fought among each other for control of small stretches of territory. The Byzantines were unable to gain control over all of Algeria, and their custom of levying heavy taxes on the people to pay for the armies used to police the towns added to their unpopularity.

A NEW FAITH

The next invaders to enter North Africa were the armies of Uqba ibn Nafi al-Fihri. Approximately 50 years after the death of the Prophet Muhammad, his followers had spread the religion he had founded, Islam, across much of the Arabian Peninsula and were now carrying it from Egypt to North Africa. These Arab warriors converted many of the Christian Berbers, winning their support and successfully driving out any remnants of Byzantine culture.

The alliance between the Arabs and the Berbers, however, was uneasy and did not last. While willing converts to Islam, the Berbers were less willing to accept other elements of Arab culture. The Berbers viewed the Arabs as brutal and arrogant, while the Arabs—like the Greeks and Romans before them— viewed the Berbers as barbaric. Arab control was strongest in the larger coastal towns along the Mediterranean. Farther from the coast, the Berbers remained more loyal to their own tribes than to Arab rule.

Arab rule was centered on Abd al-Rahman ibn Rustam and his successors, who established an Islamic kingdom in Algeria and ruled it from 761 to 909. This was a brief "golden age" of Islamic rule in Algeria. The Rustamids, as they are known, were famous for their study of math and astronomy as well as their support for the development of the arts. Their courts were considered to be models of justice and equality. The Rustamids, however, were far less successful at maintaining their army. For the next 600 years, control of Algeria shifted from one group to another. During the rule of the Berber Zirids (972–1148), when Algeria became the center of regional power, the city of Algiers was founded. For more than half a century, power shifted from the Zirids to the Hammadits to the Almoravids to the Almohads and to the Zianids. The period was marked by disputes over religious practices, corruption, and violent rebellions. Gradually, the once-mighty territory that had encompassed much of North Africa dissolved into smaller regions or kingdoms, known as the Barbary States.

PIRATES ON THE MEDITERRANEAN

By the 1400s, Islamic rule had extended into the Iberian Peninsula, portions of the land we know today as the nations of Portugal and Spain. Spanish rulers Ferdinand and Isabella were determined to seize back these lands, and, by 1492, they had pushed Islamic armies out of Spain and even controlled portions of North Africa. They then established Spanish forts along the coast, including at Oran, Tlemcen, and Algiers, where ships that wanted to trade along that route were required to pay fees for the right to use Spanish-held waterways.

For much of the sixteenth and seventeenth centuries, Algeria and the other portions of North Africa—the Barbary States—became notorious havens for pirates. These Barbary pirates attacked ships attempting to sail along the southern Mediterranean, seizing cargo and charging governments steep fees in order to allow other ships to pass through safely. Algiers became a city whose economy was dependent on pirate activity, and shops specialized in the resale of goods seized by piracy.

Among these Barbary pirates—or *corsairs*, as they were sometimes called—were a group of brothers who had been born in a region that is now part of Greece. They became sailors and traders, skilled in the languages of the many different ports they visited. The oldest brother was named Aroudj (sometimes spelled Arudj). The brothers might have continued as successful traders had Aroudj not been captured by members of the Knights of St. John, Crusaders who were seizing trading vessels and any non-Christian ship to curtail the spread of Islam through the Middle East and North Africa. Aroudj was held captive for three years. Accounts vary as to whether he spent those three years in the dungeon of a castle in Turkey or as a slave on a galley ship.

After his brothers finally rescued him, Aroudj vowed vengeance on those who had held him captive. He was determined to wage war against the ships that were controlled or protected by the Knights of St. John. An Egyptian prince who was willing to help him in his campaign of terror provided him with money in exchange for a share of any loot taken from captured ships.

BARBARY PIRATES AND THOMAS JEFFERSON

For several centuries, pirates from the regions we know today as Algeria, Tunisia, and Morocco—then called the Barbary States—roamed the waters of the Mediterranean, seizing ships and kidnapping victims for ransom. Major naval powers were forced to pay them a fee, or "tribute," in order to guarantee safe passage for their ships.

After the United States won its independence from Great Britain in 1783, it too was forced to negotiate with these pirates. In the first years after independence, the U.S. Congress designated $80,000 as a tribute to the Barbary pirates. Two future U.S. presidents, Thomas Jefferson and John Adams, then serving as diplomats in Europe, were ordered to negotiate with the pirates to ensure the safety of American ships. Jefferson was especially outraged at the idea of negotiating with pirates. While in Paris, he attempted to form a confederation with several European powers to prevent the payment of any fees to the pirates and to force them to bring an end to their activities.

Aroudj was joined by two of his brothers, Isaac and Kheir-ed-din. The brothers soon became legendary in the Mediterranean for their daring attacks on ships far larger and better armed than the small vessels in which they were sailing. They even captured two large papal galley ships (ships that were part of the naval fleet controlled by the pope) loaded with treasures.[1] As Aroudj added new ships to his pirate fleet with each successful attack, more men came under his direction. Soon, with more than a dozen ships involved in each attack,

Jefferson's plan would have involved the formation of an international naval force that would patrol the Mediterranean to protect ships in those waters. He was able to interest Portugal, Naples, Sicily, Venice, Denmark, Sweden, and Malta in the plan, but Spain had just paid a huge fee to the pirate states and felt that its ships were now sufficiently protected. The plans collapsed amid concerns that Great Britain or France might decide to support the pirates.

Jefferson, bitterly disappointed, was convinced that paying tributes would only lead to additional demands. In 1795 alone, the United States paid nearly $1 million in cash and supplies. The nation even gave a frigate to the pirates.

After Jefferson became president in 1801, he refused to continue paying outrageous sums in protection money. The United States quickly found itself in armed combat with the Barbary States. The fighting lasted for nearly four years, until the United States signed a treaty that brought an end to the hostilities. Payments were still periodically made to the pirates by the United States until 1815; European nations continued to make payments until the 1830s.

In this painting, Barbary pirates attack Spanish ships. From the sixteenth century onward, Barbary pirates, also known as Barbary corsairs, operating out of modern-day Algeria attacked European shipping lanes and captured thousands of people. The piracy was not completely suppressed until the French occupation of Algeria in 1830.

Aroudj developed a strategy of stringing his pirate ships in a line, close enough so that each ship was within viewing range of the ships on its left and right. Any vessel that attempted to cross the line could swiftly be captured.

It was not long before these attacks drew the fury of the famed Spanish Armada. Aroudj did his best to avoid any direct engagements with the Spanish fleet, instead targeting the smaller, less heavily armed vessels belonging to Italian states that routinely sailed the Mediterranean, such as Genoa, Sicily, Naples, and Tuscany. These ships were normally loaded with goods for trade; the sailors could be captured and turned into slaves, while the goods were seized and taken to Algiers. But on one occasion, in the Algerian city of Bougie, Aroudj and his men came into range of the Spanish and were quickly targeted in a fierce volley of cannon fire. Aroudj and his men barely escaped; he lost his arm as a result of wounds inflicted by a cannonball.

While Aroudj and his fleet lacked the might and firepower of the Spanish Armada, they did have something in common with many of the people in the port cities of Algeria: their faith. Spain's success under King Ferdinand and Queen Isabella in banishing Islam from Spanish territory and their efforts to do the same in North Africa had sparked bitter resentment among the Berbers, who had converted to Islam years before, and the Arabs, who had brought that faith to the region. Secretly and not so secretly, these people began supporting Aroudj and his brothers in their efforts to plunder Christian ships passing through the waters.

PIRATE KINGDOM

By the early 1500s, Aroudj had become a wealthy man. His reputation had spread through many of the port cities of Algeria. Often the leaders of these port towns would seek his assistance in dealing with issues involving trade, shipping, or problems sparked by conflicts with the Spanish.

The new twist in Aroudj's career came when he seized a Sicilian ship loaded with wheat and then landed with this booty at the small port town of Djidjelli, approximately 180 miles (290 kilometers) east of Algiers. The people of Djidjelli had been suffering through a famine, and Aroudj was hailed as a hero for arriving with grain just as the people were facing starvation. They pleaded with the pirate to become their "king."[2]

Djidjelli would provide the base for a far more ambitious campaign. The death of King Ferdinand of Spain in 1516 prompted many local rulers in North Africa, eager to retake their territories, to claim that any oaths they had taken swearing loyalty to the king of Spain were no longer valid now that

Ferdinand had died. This was the case in Algiers, where the Arab sheik who ruled the town invited Aroudj and his pirates to join the campaign to drive the Spanish out of Algiers.

Aroudj began his campaign with a stop in Cherchell (called Caesarea in Roman times). Cherchell was a coastal town located about 150 miles (240 kilometers) west of Algiers, whose inhabitants were mainly Muslim refugees from Spain. One of Aroudj's men had taken command of the town and named himself its king. Aroudj was not happy with this demonstration of independence. He landed at Cherchell and demanded a meeting with his former deputy. When the man arrived for the meeting, Aroudj cut off his head. Aroudj then rounded up as many of the able-bodied men that he could find in the town. Leaving behind only a few as guards, he loaded the rest onto his ships and sailed for Algiers.

In Algiers, he and his men engaged in fierce fighting with the Spanish, but they were unable to force them from the city. Instead, Aroudj turned his attention to the sheik who had first summoned him there. He strangled the sheik, then announced to the people that he would be their new "king." Soon, he discovered that some leaders in Algiers were trying to negotiate with the Spanish to drive out Aroudj and his men. Aroudj summoned the men involved in the plot to a mosque. Once they had gathered, he drew aside the wealthiest, most influential man who had been involved and executed him in front of the others. There were no further attempts to force Aroudj out of Algiers.

Despite this brutal behavior, other towns continued to call on Aroudj and his brothers for assistance in dealing with problems involving local rule. Aroudj decided to leave his younger brother, Kheir-ed-din, in charge of Algiers while he and a third brother, Isaac, led a fleet of men westward to the towns of Tenez and Tlemcen, where their support had been requested. There they were successful in securing control of both towns as well as several others that dotted the coast.

The son of the sheik that Aroudj had murdered in Algiers was determined that his father's murderer would not simply sail away to greater glory and power. He complained to the local Spanish representative in the region, who was increasingly alarmed at Aroudj's success in gaining control of the many port cities critical to trade along the North African coast. He sent an urgent message to the new king of Spain, Charles V, asking that the king send an army to stamp out Aroudj and bring North Africa back under Spanish control. King Charles V responded, sending the requested troops in 1518.

In the fierce fighting that followed, both Aroudj and Isaac (as well as most of their men) were killed. Only a few survivors were able to make their way back to Algiers to inform Kheir-ed-din of his brothers' fate and warn him that the Spanish were sailing for Algiers to force him out as well.

BARBAROSSA AND THE OTTOMANS

Kheir-ed-din was devastated by the news of his brothers' deaths. He also knew that his small force would be no match for the Spanish army. He turned to the only neighboring power strong enough and willing enough to help him fight off the Spanish: the Ottoman Empire. At the time, the Ottomans were slowly building an empire that would span much of the Middle East and Eastern Europe within the next century. Kheir-ed-din sent a messenger to the sultan of the Ottoman Empire, asking for military aid and offering, in exchange, Algiers as a province.

The sultan, Selim I, agreed. Kheir-ed-din received money, cannons, and 2,400 warriors. Algiers became an Ottoman province, with Kheir-ed-din its governor. (It would remain under Turkish control for 300 years, until 1830.) The Turkish warriors soon began expanding that province, eventually ensuring that much of North Africa fell under Ottoman control. Kheir-ed-din, who became known as Barbarossa (Red Beard), quickly reinforced the fortifications at Algiers in preparation of a Spanish attack.

The sixteenth-century sailor and pirate Barbarossa is today considered one of the founders of Algeria, as he sought to create a Muslim kingdom in the center of North Africa.

But the attack did not come when expected. As a Spanish fleet of 40 ships gathered off Algiers waiting for reinforcements to arrive, a fierce storm struck. It ultimately capsized more than half of the Spanish ships and destroyed most of their supplies.

Barbarossa's forces, accompanied by local Berbers, swept in while the Spanish forces were desperately trying to reassemble. They then seized the remaining supplies and enslaved much of the Spanish force. More than 3,000 soldiers and 36 officers were captured on the Algerian coast; many more were killed.[3]

This defeat of the Spanish cemented Barbarossa's power and Ottoman control in the region. Soon, Barbarossa's pirates were expanding their attacks farther west, to the Spanish provinces of Valencia and Catalonia and to the islands located in the western Mediterranean. The Spanish were pushed into a defensive position. They built forts and watchtowers along the Spanish coast to counter the ongoing attacks from pirate ships.

Meanwhile, Barbarossa focused on establishing and expanding a Muslim "kingdom" in the center of North Africa. Gradually, he expanded control into more remote regions farther from the coast. It was a challenging task; the Berbers he encountered had their own tribal leaders and no desire to place themselves under outside control. The one advantage Barbarossa offered was that he was neither Spanish nor Christian; the violent dominance of the Spanish had won them few friends in that part of the world. Many in the more remote regions of Algeria were willing to join his army when the stated goal became the reconquest of North Africa and Spain under the banner of Islam.

The Ottoman ruler was so grateful for Barbarossa's efforts that he summoned him to the Ottoman capital, Constantinople (today Istanbul). In 1533, he named Barbarossa admiral of the Ottoman fleet. For the next 14 years, until his death in 1547, Barbarossa led a series of successful naval raids on Italy, Nice, Majorca, and Tunis at the head of the Ottoman fleet. Algeria became the base from which Ottoman raids were launched. Such raids gradually placed more territory in North Africa under Ottoman control. This control, however, was light; North African provinces paid tribute to the empire but often acted independently. Algeria was governed by a *dey*, an administrative chief (generally a military official) elected in Turkey. But the economy remained heavily dependent on piracy throughout the latter sixteenth and early seventeenth centuries. Money came not just from the ships and cargo that were seized but also from wealthy Europeans who were kidnapped and held for ransom.

Algeria was the center of Ottoman power in North Africa. As Ottoman control extended out from Algiers into more remote areas in the region, Algeria began to take shape as a unique territory, separate from the other Ottoman territories in North Africa—Constantine, Mascara, and Titteri. The Ottomans collected taxes in Algeria and, as they expanded their military, built relationships with local tribal leaders who supplied men in exchange for special privileges. The Ottomans maintained control over towns, roads, and ports. People wishing to trade in the marketplace or work in the Ottoman lands needed a special permit to do so.

It was during this period that Algeria began to exist as a specific region for the first time in its history, even though Ottoman control was stronger in the major cities of the north than it was in the more remote regions to the south. This period of Ottoman dominance would be viewed by future generations of Algerians in idealized terms as a time of "independence," when Algeria was a unified country operating under an Islamic government. The truth is, of course, more complicated. When the Ottoman Empire began to weaken in the early 1800s, its control over Algeria also weakened. Tribal leaders became bolder in their efforts to reclaim land and in their refusal to pay the hated taxes.

Perhaps more significantly, European navies—particularly those of the British and Dutch—were now powerful enough to begin to beat back the piracy that had plagued the Mediterranean for so long. Algeria became increasingly dependent on trade with France to keep its economy thriving; for example, it supplied a considerable amount of grain to the armies of Napoleon Bonaparte as they fought in Italy and seized territory in Egypt. It was this trading relationship—and a disagreement between diplomats—that would bring the French military to Algiers in 1830 and begin an experiment in colonization that would last more than a century.

The French Arrive

I t began with an insult and a diplomatic crisis. It ended with
Algeria once more under foreign control—a control that
would last 132 years.

There are differing versions about precisely what triggered
the arrival of French troops off the coast of Algeria. In one
popular version, it was an unpaid debt. At the end of the eigh-
teenth century and in the early part of the nineteenth century,
Algeria had developed an important trade relationship with
France. Large quantities of Algerian grain were shipped to
the southern provinces of France, where they supplied those
armies of Napoleon Bonaparte that were fighting in Italy and
Egypt. The French were slow to pay, and gradually the debt for
the grain grew to nearly 8 million francs.

In April 1827, the French diplomat at Algiers, Pierre Deval,
arranged a visit to the dey, the chief Ottoman administrator. The

occasion was a celebration marking the feast at the end of the month-long Islamic fast of Ramadan. In this account of the diplomatic incident, Hussein Dey asked why the French king had not responded to his letters that inquired about the settlement of the outstanding debt. Deval responded somewhat haughtily that the French king could not be expected to communicate directly with the dey. A furious Hussein Dey responded by hitting Deval three times on the arm with the handle of a peacock-feather fly swatter and ordering him to leave.[1]

Another account suggests that Hussein Dey was testy after a long day of fasting in observance of Ramadan and was not terribly welcoming and gracious when Deval first arrived. This supposedly prompted Deval to respond in a similar manner, and the two diplomats were soon exchanging heated words. All the accounts conclude in the same way, however, with Hussein striking the French diplomat with a fly swatter. Hussein's letter to the Ottoman sultan, Mahmud II, confirms this. He stated that Deval's offensive words inspired him to hit the French representative with "light blows" two or three times with the fly swatter he held in his "humble hand."[2]

Regardless of the trigger, Deval was quick to report the incident to his superiors in France. Napoleon had been ousted, and the monarchy had been restored in 1814. But the new king, Charles X, had been ruler for only a few years and was eager to cement his power and to add to his reputation with a decisive demonstration of force.

In mid-June 1827, a French naval squadron appeared off the coast of Algiers with a series of demands. The representatives wanted an official apology and demanded that the fleur-de-lis—the symbol of the French monarchy—be flown over the Qasba (also spelled Casbah), the citadel that served as a fortress protecting Algiers, and honored with a 100-gun salute.

As the official representative of the Ottoman Empire in Algiers, the dey refused. Pierre Deval and the others who staffed the French consulate quickly boarded the French ship and then announced a blockade of Algiers. Hussein Dey responded by ordering the destruction of French trading posts in the cities of Bône and La Calle.

THE CONFLICT BUILDS

France added more ships to support the blockade—first four, then seven, then a dozen, until finally 18 ships were blocking access to Algiers. The standoff stretched into 1828 without successfully forcing Algerian capitulation. Finally, King Charles X—whose policies were becoming increasingly unpopular in France—ordered a diplomat to travel to Algiers to negotiate some sort of settlement to the standoff. The diplomat

CHARLES X

Charles X of France was born on October 9, 1757, at the palace of Versailles in France. The members of the French royal family known as the Bourbon dynasty lived in dangerous times, as France passed from revolution to empire to monarchy, and their periods on the throne tended to be short-lived. Proof of this is that two of Charles X's older brothers served as king before the throne became his.

In fact, it had once seemed unlikely that Charles would be king of France, since he had four older brothers ahead of him in line for the throne. Prior to the French Revolution, he was given the title of Comte d'Artois. When the revolution began, he fled France for England, where he stayed until 1814, when the monarchy was restored in France. For this reason, this historical period is called the Restoration.

Two of Charles's older brothers had died, a third was guillotined, and the fourth became heir to the throne provided the dey with the French proposal. However, as he was leaving Algiers, his ship was fired upon from the port.

Charles X was furious. He fired his moderate prime minister and appointed a far more conservative one in his stead, Jules de Polignac. This further alienated French citizens, who were dissatisfied with this heavy-handed demonstration of royal power and with the increasingly expensive and embarrassing failures in Algiers.

Polignac had been heavily influenced by foreign policy in Great Britain at the time.[3] Britain was building an impressive empire, with colonies in various parts of the globe. Polignac recognized that Britain's empire was expanding in the Middle

when his 10-year-old nephew died in prison. This fourth brother, who became King Louis XVIII in 1814 when France restored the monarchy, ruled for 10 years prior to his death on September 16, 1824. Charles then took the throne and became King Charles X.

Seeking to demonstrate his control as king of France, Charles X introduced a number of policies that quickly made him highly unpopular. He appointed the very conservative Jules Armand de Polignac as prime minister; it was Polignac who helped spearhead the French efforts to colonize Algeria. Charles X's efforts to restrict freedom of the press and voting rights, and to limit the power of the legislature, led to revolts in the streets. Charles X was forced to abdicate the throne in July 1830. He had planned to abdicate in favor of his grandson, but instead Charles X's cousin seized power and dubbed himself King Louis Philippe.

Charles X fled to England and then moved to the regions we now know as the Czech Republic and Slovenia. He died in Slovenia on November 6, 1836.

Under the unpopular French king Charles X, French forces conquered Algeria in 1830. Charles used an insult to a French diplomat and continuing piracy as grounds to occupy Algeria.

East, Africa, and Asia. He saw an opportunity for France to expand its empire closer to home—in fact, just across the Mediterranean, in Algeria. He also sensed that a decisive and forceful military victory in Algeria would help sway public opinion back in support of the monarchy.

The French were helped by the fact that the piracy that had plagued shipping in the Mediterranean—much of it stemming from Algeria—had alienated many foreign powers, who were more than willing to let France establish a strong and law-abiding presence in Algeria. On March 2, 1830, King Charles X announced, "I can no longer allow to go unpunished the grave insult to my flag; the resounding redress that I hope to obtain in satisfying the honor of France will with the Almighty's help turn to the profit of Christendom."[4]

The king had portrayed the invasion of Algeria as protecting the honor of France and as a battle of Christianity versus Islam. France assembled an impressive military force of more than 34,000 soldiers and 3,300 noncombatants in a fleet of 635 ships.[5] The force set sail across the Mediterranean on May 25, 1830, urged on by a cheering crowd. The fleet reached Algerian shores on May 31, but rough weather forced the ships to anchor in the safer harbors of Palma de Mallorca for several days. On June 14, French troops finally began landing on Algerian soil. For five days, French forces established a perimeter, unloaded their supplies and military gear, and set up a large camp.

Watching these events in alarm, the dey had ordered his son-in-law, Agha Ibrahim, to muster a defensive force to protect Algiers from invasion. The Algerian forces (recall that Algiers was still considered Ottoman territory, and the Ottoman Empire was based in Turkey) included 7,000 Turks as well as an additional 26,000 Algerian troops.[6] The Algerians had an advantage in their rifles and in the skill of their marksmen, but their artillery was inferior to that of the French. Additionally, they were more poorly supplied and led.

While the French were setting up their base camp, they came under only sporadic fire from the Algerian troops. When the Algerians led a more decisive attack on June 19, the French had already been able to establish secure positions. Eventually, the French forced the Ottoman army back into Algiers. That city then became the target for French troops on June 29. As they marched from the coast into the city, the French distributed propaganda in Arabic intended to reassure the people of Algeria that their intent was merely to liberate Algerians from the Ottoman Empire. But the destruction perpetrated by French troops as they marched toward the city left the Algerians doubting the peaceful intent of the invaders. When the French reached the outskirts of the city, panicked Algerians began fleeing Algiers by the thousands. They headed for boats or raced to the south and east, away from the invading army.

On July 5, 1830, the last Ottoman diplomat in Algiers signed the formal terms of surrender, and the white flag of Charles X was raised over the Qasba at noon on that day. The terms of surrender included the transfer of the Qasba, all forts, and the port of Algiers to French troops. The French troops promised to allow Algerians the continued free practice of the Muslim religion; the people of Algiers would also be free to retain their property and their businesses. Immediately, however, French troops—in direct violation of the terms of surrender—began rampaging through the streets of Algiers, attacking people and destroying their homes, businesses, and places of worship. Much of the city was devastated, setting a pattern of violence that would plague France's efforts to occupy Algeria for more than a century.

It would take three years before the French parliament, pressured because of reports of great violence during the occupation of Algeria, sent a formal parliamentary commission to investigate. Its report, issued in 1834, noted:

> We have sent to their deaths on simple suspicion and without trial people whose guilt was always doubtful. . . . We massa-

cred people carrying [our] safe conducts, slaughtered on suspicion entire populations subsequently found to be innocent
. . . we have rewarded treason in the name of negotiation, and
termed diplomatic action odious acts of entrapment.[7]

The report disclosed the fact that French troops had destroyed
cemeteries, seized property, occupied privately owned homes
and buildings, and turned mosques into military barracks.

OCCUPATION

The French occupation of Algeria began, at least in part, as a
way to rally the people of France behind their king. In this it
failed. Charles X's efforts to curtail freedom of the press, restrict
voting rights, and dissolve more liberal branches of government sparked public outrage and violence in France. In July
1830, he was forced to abdicate and flee France; his cousin,
Louis Philippe, became king.

Despite the change in monarch, the occupation of Algeria
continued, as it was now declared a matter of national prestige
and honor. King Louis Philippe decided by 1834 that the occupied territory of Algeria should be annexed. A French military
governor-general was appointed in July 1834 to oversee the
government of this newly declared French colony, then loosely
labeled "French possessions in the north of Africa." It was not
until 1839, however, that the French minister of war formally
referred to the colony by the name Algeria. This fact would later
be used by opponents of Algerian independence as evidence
that the country of Algeria was actually a French creation, a territory carved out of tribal areas and unoccupied land.[8]

There was, of course, resistance to the early French efforts
to colonize Algeria. Initially, the main source of that resistance
was a 25-year-old religious figure, Abd el-Kader, whose followers believed that he descended directly from the Prophet
Muhammad. A member of the Qadiriya religious order, Abd el-
Kader described resistance against the French invaders as a holy

Abd el-Kader was a military, political, and religious leader who led Algerians in a struggle against the French in the 1830s and 1840s. Some Algerians regard him as their national hero.

war. He was so successful at organizing and leading resistance against French forces that he was ultimately recognized as a leader and official representative of the Algerians by the French, who finally agreed to sign a treaty with him to bring an end to his campaign of violent resistance.

For the French, the most valuable parts of Algeria were Algiers and the northern port cities. In the Treaty of Tafna, signed in 1837, Abd el-Kader was recognized by the French as the ruler of much of western and inland central Algeria. They also recognized him as the ruler of an area stretching from Biskra to the Moroccan border in the south and from the Kabylie region east of Algiers to Oran in the north. All of this territory encompassed approximately two-thirds of Algeria.[9]

The treaty was initially designed to create two loose entities—an Arab territory and a French territory—but the actual borders and boundaries of these two territories were left vague, and almost inevitably, conflict broke out once more. The French were determined to cement their control over the region, and so Marshal Thomas-Robert Bugeaud was dispatched to stamp out any resistance to the establishment of a French colony.

FRESH WATER AND FERTILE LAND

Marshal Bugeaud was a war hero who, in 1831, became marshal (much like a general) of the French army. He had fought in the Napoleonic wars and, during campaigns in Spain, had become an expert on guerrilla warfare. He was responsible for maintaining order in Paris during public protests in 1834 (many of the methods he used for dealing with riots were later criticized for being excessively harsh) and was then dispatched to Algeria.

Bugeaud championed a new military strategy in Algeria. He would replace huge and cumbersome units with smaller and more mobile ones that could track enemies over rough and remote territory quickly. Bugeaud was determined to place colonizers throughout Algeria. In a speech to France's National

Assembly in 1840, he made this clear: "Wherever there is fresh water and fertile land, there one must locate *colons* [colonizers], without concerning oneself to whom these lands belong."[10] Bugeaud, moreover, communicated this attitude to the soldiers under his command. French troops routinely devastated the communities and people they encountered, seizing property and brutally killing any Algerians who got in their way.

As a symbol of Algerian resistance to the French colonization of Algeria, Abd el-Kader became the target of Bugeaud's campaign. The French commander mobilized more than 100,000 French troops in Algeria, one-third of the French army. The army was given instructions to follow a "scorched-earth policy." Villages suspected of aiding Abd el-Kader were burned, their crops destroyed. As a result, these now-starving and homeless people were forced to abandon their communities. French colonizers then moved in to seize the land and build their own settlements there.

These two men—Marshal Bugeaud and Abd el-Kader—became respectively the symbols of French colonization and Algerian resistance in the early days of France's occupation of Algeria. Abd el-Kader would serve as an inspiration for Algerian nationalists for more than a century; Bugeaud would be heralded as the founder of the French state of Algeria. For more than six years, they battled for control of Algeria, with the French steadily pushing back Algerian forces and driving native people from their homes.

In the end, however, Abd el-Kader was pushed farther and farther west to the border of Morocco. In the hills above Oujda, he finally surrendered on December 23, 1847. (That same year, for his success in conquering much of Algeria, Bugeaud was named Algeria's governor-general.) Abd el-Kader was held in prison in France until 1852. Upon release, he moved to Syria. There, in the capital city of Damascus, he helped to abort a planned massacre of Christians in 1860, saving an estimated

12,000 lives, including that of the French consul. He spent the rest of his life in exile, dying in Damascus in 1883. His remains were finally brought back to Algeria in 1966 to mark the one hundred and thirty-sixth anniversary of the French invasion of Algeria.

A French Colony

From its earliest years as a French colony, Algeria was shattered by conflict—not simply between the French settlers and the Algerians, but also between the settlers and the politicians in France who shaped policies that impacted life in Algeria. The problem stemmed in part from the political instability in France at the time. French attitudes toward Algeria were greatly influenced by whoever happened to be in power in Paris.

For decades after the start of the French Revolution in 1789, the French government veered back and forth between a monarchy and a republic. In 1848, shortly after Algeria firmly came under French control, the monarchy in France collapsed and France again became a republic—the Second Republic (the government during the French Revolution is today viewed as the First Republic). During the Second Republic's brief period in power (1848–1851), the French leaders announced their plan to "assimilate" Algeria and give it political representatives in France.

But political rivals quickly challenged the leaders of the Second Republic, and any thoughts of a more democratic approach in Algeria were extinguished as the Republic struggled simply to survive. Ever since Marshal Bugeaud had

THE WRETCHED OF THE EARTH

From the opening pages of Frantz Fanon's *The Wretched of the Earth*, the author offers a biting condemnation of France's efforts to block Algerian liberation and a stern rebuttal to the excuses and delays that had limited Algerian efforts toward self-government, as shown in the excerpt below:

> Decolonization, which sets out to change the order of the world, is clearly an agenda for total disorder. But it cannot be accomplished by the wave of a magic wand, a natural cataclysm, or a gentleman's agreement. Decolonization, we know, is an historical process: In other words, it can only be understood, it can only find its significance and become self coherent insofar as we can discern the history-making movement which gives it form and substance. . . . The colonist and the colonized are old acquaintances. And consequently, the colonist is right when he says he "knows" them. It is the colonist who *fabricated* and *continues to fabricate* the colonized subject. The colonist derives his validity, i.e. his wealth, from the colonial system.*

* Frantz Fanon (trans. by Richard Philcox), *The Wretched of the Earth*. New York: Grove Press, 2004, p. 2.

expanded and cemented French control over much of Algeria, the French army rather than the French parliament had administered the territory. To this end, France's Foreign Legion was formed in 1831. Its headquarters were at Sidi-Bel-Abbès, south of Oran.

The French army quickly adopted many of the same structures originally set up by the Ottoman Empire in Algeria. Relationships were established with friendly tribal leaders, tax collectors, and judges, who would oversee a system of collecting taxes from the local people to support the French military presence. In exchange, these friendly tribal leaders, tax collectors, and judges were given a share of the harvests and taxes collected. Also, the army in 1844 created a Bureau of Arab Affairs, the goal of which was to build better relationships with the local people. Officers spoke Arabic and were familiar with local customs. Their approach, however, was based upon the philosophy that French culture and customs were inherently superior and that the local people needed to be educated and "civilized."

AN ARAB KINGDOM

By 1849, approximately 35,000 French settlers were living in Algeria.[1] They strongly resisted any talk of representation for native Algerians in the French parliament. Instead, they felt that the only way to successfully build French settlements in Algeria was to suppress the native people.

In December 1851, Louis-Napoleon Bonaparte, the nephew of the former French emperor Napoleon Bonaparte, overthrew the Second Republic of France. A new empire—the Second Empire—was declared, and Louis-Napoleon soon became Emperor Napoleon III. Napoleon III's attitude toward Algeria shifted during his time in power. At first, he spoke of his belief that Algeria was an extension of French territory. By 1860, he had made a dramatic shift, describing his idea of an Arab kingdom, his love for Arab culture, and his plan for bringing about reconciliation between the French and Arab communities in Algeria. In his vision, of course, he would be the king of the Arabs. This was a highly unpopular view among French settlers in Algeria, who became strong supporters of efforts to overthrow Napoleon III and establish a new republic in France.

Despite Napoleon III's later statements, policies were enacted in Algeria during the Second Empire that made it increasingly difficult to envision equality among the different peoples living in Algeria. European settlers, mostly French but also Italian and Spanish, had already seized great stretches of territory and took further steps to eliminate local culture. The Grand Mosque, or Djemaa el-Kebir, of Algiers was one of the symbols of this. The site of the Djemaa el-Kebir had been a holy one from Algiers's earliest history, when Berbers and Phoenicians built a place of prayer there. Later, it became a Roman temple and then a Christian basilica. The mosque was built there in the eleventh century, its minaret rising high into the sky. Under French rule, it became the Cathedral of Saint Philippe, and a cross was placed atop the minaret.

In 1865, the French government passed new laws that seemed on the surface to be a protection for religious practices and local customs. Under these laws, Algerians were treated as "subjects" rather than "citizens." Muslims would be governed by Islamic law; decisions in legal matters would be made by Muslim judges (*cadis*) rather than according to French civil law. In order to become French citizens, Muslims had to give up the right to be governed by Islamic law. For many, this amounted to a renunciation of their faith. This created a fundamental gap between the citizen and subject, the latter of whom had no say in determining the laws and policies that governed daily life in Algeria.

This gap between citizen and subject became even sharper in 1870, when a new law gave citizenship to Algeria's Jewish population but *not* the Muslim majority. It was a time of discontent in Algeria; the Second Empire had collapsed and been replaced by a republic (the Third Republic). Although deputies

The Grand Mosque of Algiers is seen here in a photograph from around 1890. During Algeria's time as a French colony, this eleventh-century mosque was converted into a Christian cathedral by the French.

in the French national assembly now represented Algeria, only those Algerians who were considered French citizens were able to vote for deputies.

Around this time, a Muslim leader named El-Mokhrani called for a *jihad*, or holy war, against French rule. Although some 800,000 Muslims rallied to his side, El-Mokhrani lacked military skill or experience in command, and the rebellion quickly failed. The French then moved swiftly to deal with those suspected of aiding the rebels. Vast stretches of tribal lands were seized, and tribal leaders were forced out of Algeria. Following the uprising, native culture came under direct attack. Arabic was officially categorized as a foreign language in Algeria, Islamic religious schools were placed under surveillance, and pilgrimages to Mecca (which practitioners of Islam believe all Muslims must perform at least once in their lives) were tightly controlled.[2]

In response to the rebellion, French settlers were given even greater support by the government in Paris, which encouraged them to spread French culture and values to all areas of Algeria. Northern Algeria was formally divided into three French departments in 1881; the Sahara and southern regions were kept under the control of the French army. Many French viewed these southern regions as uncivilized, a frontier kept under control only by the courageous efforts of the Foreign Legion.

Each of the three departments sent two representatives to the National Assembly in Paris, but only "full French citizens" (adult, male, non-Muslim settlers) had the right to vote. Moreover, the three councils established to regulate these departments were set up in such a way as to discriminate against Muslims. Elected settlers made up four-fifths of the membership; the remaining fifth contained Muslim landowners who had been selected by French authorities. Local councils, even in areas that were predominantly Muslim, were designed in such a way that Muslim representatives could never exceed one-quarter; most were appointed by the French administration.[3]

In 1881, the legal system reinforced this widespread discrimination with the passage of the Code de l'Indigénat (Code of the Native People). This code was designed to place even greater restrictions on the Muslim people. It was now a crime to make disrespectful remarks about the Third Republic or to be rude to a colonial official. It was a crime not to answer questions from an official, to travel without a permit, or to forget to declare a family birth. The code contained a total of 33 "crimes," which were not illegal in France but were considered punishable offenses in Algeria.

The French settlers who rushed to Algeria at the end of the nineteenth century were, for the most part, not wealthy or highly educated. Instead, they saw in Algeria an opportunity to enjoy a status far superior to what they could experience in their homeland. This, of course, made them even more determined to preserve the distinct class structure between French citizens (citizenship was extended to settlers from Spain, Italy, and Malta in 1889) and the Muslim population. The French settlers were so poor that some even arrived barefoot in Algeria, giving rise to the term *pied noir*, meaning "black foot."

The Warnier law of 1873 dictated that communally held land—generally, land that was held by a tribe—would be divided into individual lots so that it could be sold more easily. Between 1871 and 1898, French settlers acquired 1 million hectares (2.5 million acres) of land.[4] The best agricultural lands were always given to French settlers.

DIVIDE AND CONQUER

Discrimination was also clear in the policy of taxation. The French maintained a system of taxes that had first been collected under Ottoman rule—these were called "Arab taxes." They included a tax that required the payment of a tithe, or share, of the harvest from certain key crops as well as a tax on camels, horses, cattle, sheep, and goats. They also included a tax that was supposed to support the maintenance of roads and public services, such as schools. (Despite such taxation, schools used by native Algerian children were poorly equipped and poorly funded.)

In addition to these "Arab taxes," Algerians were also expected to pay French taxes, which included taxes on undeveloped and developed land, fees for licenses to entitle someone to perform certain trades or jobs, rent taxes, customs duties, taxes on tobacco and other goods, and other registration fees. In order to encourage settlement, European immigrants were exempted from the "Arab taxes" and many of the French taxes

In this hand-colored photograph from the late nineteenth century, a group of native Algerians engage in a conversation on a street in Algeria. During the French colonial period, native Algerians did not have the same rights as French citizens living in Algeria or their Algerian-born children.

as well. According to one estimate, native Algerians by 1912 owned 38 percent of the land and goods of the colony but paid more than 71 percent of the taxes.[5]

As European settlers married and had families, a new dynamic began to unfold: More and more of the people known as colons, or European settlers, were actually born in Algeria. This created a new division. Those who had been born in Algeria and descended from European settlers enjoyed special rights and privileges, while those who also had been born in Algeria but descended from Arabs, Berbers, or other "native" groups were discriminated against. This was clearest in the cities of northern Algeria, where the greatest percentage of European settlers had originally made their homes.

In 1926, the number of colons was 833,000. In 1931, they comprised 69 percent of the total population in Algiers, 79 percent in Oran, 48 percent in Constantine, and 57 percent in Bône. Of these people, an overwhelming 79 percent had been born on Algerian soil.[6] Over the next three decades, these numbers would shift dramatically. While the population of European descendants remained fairly consistent, the number of Muslims in Algeria began to grow—and they increasingly moved to the cities. By 1954, the population of the city of Oran

INJUSTICE AND PREJUDICE

The French colonization of Algeria was marked by a strong prejudice against those who had lived there before the arrival of European settlers. Laws and the systems of education and taxation highlighted the divide and demonstrated this bias against Algerians. This prejudice was not unique to the French; it was a view widely shared by many Europeans. Anthony Wilkin, an Englishman who traveled to Algeria at the end of the nineteenth century and published an account of his travels in 1900, *Among the Berbers of Algeria*, demonstrates this bias in language that is shocking today:

> It is not a hundred years since Algiers constituted at once a menace and a disgrace to European civilization, since its corsairs infested the seas and swept together into its

was 40 percent Muslim; in Algiers, Muslims made up 45 percent of the population.[7]

There were strong divisions between the two societies. Discrimination was ever present, although it was not as obvious as in, for example, the American South in the early to mid-twentieth century. There were no signs reserving certain restaurants or facilities for the French. Yet even without those signs, everyone knew of the invisible barriers that divided Algeria. On the beach just outside Algiers, one area was for those deemed French and another was for the "native" population. The areas in Algiers where European settlers lived were generally elegant, with trees lining the streets and spacious

prisons Christian sailors of every Western state . . . let us not forget that it is to the French, and to the French only, that we owe a great work of reformation—the cleansing of one of the filthiest . . . stables in the modern world. Through every change of government and of party, under King, Emperor, and Republic, at the cost of much blood and treasure, they have persisted in the work. No millions of money, no millions of sturdy colonists have rewarded these efforts. The French nation has still to endure a drain on its resources, and that with little prospect of relief. In return it enjoys a sense of possession, the use of the word "colony," and a consciousness of a great task well begun. . . .

The nomad Arab is the curse of the country. Indolent, vicious, and unprogressive, he will burn a mile of forest to provide a few acres of bad pasturage for his flocks . . . if only the destructive Arab and his locust swarms of goats could be relegated to their natural habitat—the Sahara.*

* Anthony Wilkin, *Among the Berbers of Algeria*. New York: Cassell & Company, 1900, pp. 1-4.

homes dotting the wide boulevards. Meanwhile, Muslims lived in tiny, overcrowded apartments on dark and narrow streets. The settlers' descendants used the French familiar form for the word you (*tu*) when speaking to Muslims, while Muslims were expected to address the French with the more formal and respectful *vous*. The inequality extended to schooling. As late as 1954, only 1 in 5 Muslim boys—and 1 in 16 Muslim girls—attended school.[8]

The underlying message to Algeria's Muslim population was consistent—they were inferior, held a low status, and received none of the perks and privileges granted to those whose roots were closest to France. But this attitude, which relied upon an assumption of French superiority, would soon be tested.

The Seeds of
Nationalism

The two world wars of the twentieth century contributed considerably to a radically changing view of French rule in Algeria. From 1914 to 1918, during the years of World War I, more than 173,000 Algerians fought for France and 25,000 were killed.[1] These numbers represented a significant sacrifice on the part of people who did not enjoy French citizenship or the rights and privileges of the residents of any typical French city.

To recognize this sacrifice, the French government introduced a law in 1919 to make it easier for Algerian Muslims to gain French citizenship. This law sparked violent protests among the colons, who in the decades leading up to the Algerian revolution resisted any efforts to grant the Muslims privileges that might begin to address the inequalities in

Algerian society. They had no wish to see any change in the status quo that might result in their losing their position of social and economic superiority.

In 1930, a series of elaborate celebrations were organized in Algeria to mark the hundredth anniversary of the French conquest. This was a bitter anniversary for the Muslim population; the occassion was a stark reminder of precisely how long the French had been in power on Algerian soil. Many of the festivities—including a reenactment of the landing of French forces at the beach near Algiers—demonstrated an utter disregard for the sentiment of many Algerians toward their conquerors.

The tension that had been simmering beneath the surface seemed to explode in the aftermath of these centenary celebrations. Maurice Viollette, who had served as governor-general from 1925 to 1927 and seemed far more in tune with the way many in Algeria viewed France than most of his countrymen, noted in 1931, "Before twenty years are up we will know the gravest of difficulties in North Africa."[2] Viollette immersed himself in the task of addressing this brewing problem through steps designed to lead to assimilation. By 1936, working with Prime Minister Léon Blum, he helped create reform legislation that became known as the Blum-Viollette bill. Viollette noted that his goal was that "Muslim students, while remaining Muslim, should become so French in their education, that no Frenchman, however deeply racist and religiously prejudiced he might be . . . will any longer dare to deny them French fraternity."[3]

The bill's aims were relatively modest. The bill did identify Muslims in Algeria as eligible for French citizenship, but this citizenship was to be extended to only 25,000 (out of a total of 6 million) Muslims in Algeria. The group considered eligible was among the colony's elite; academic degrees were used as one basis for deciding whether or not citizenship would be awarded. Under this bill, unlike earlier legislation, Muslims

This is a newspaper article from 1937 describing a bill by Maurice Viollette, a French politician, to give voting rotes to the native Algerians. When the French government refused to bring the plan to a vote, even moderate Algerian reformers began to desire independence from France.

could accept French citizenship without being forced to give up their rights to Islamic law.

Despite the relatively modest beginning, the Blum-Viollette bill drew violent protests from the colon community in Algeria and from their elected representatives in the French Assembly. There were speeches denouncing "liberals" in Paris who did not understand anything about Algeria. There were criticisms of Viollette for his Arab sympathies and of Blum for sponsoring a bill that threatened the way of life of French citizens in Algeria.

Prime Minister Blum had other international worries—worries that made him increasingly reluctant to adopt any policies that could threaten France's strategic position in North Africa. In 1933, Adolf Hitler and his Nazi Party had taken power in Germany and were, at the time of the Blum-Viollette bill, posing a growing threat to neighboring nations. With the government distracted by the growing Nazi menace, the Blum-Viollette bill never passed. Viollette was bitterly disappointed at the failure. He spoke before the Assembly, issuing a prophetic warning: "*Messieurs*, these men have no political nation. They do not even demand their religious nation. All they ask is to be admitted into yours. If you refuse this, beware lest they do not soon create one for themselves."[4]

This failure of the proposal poses an interesting "what if?" moment in Algerian history. At the time, in the 1930s, the Algerian Muslim population was divided. A significant number of this group favored steps that would create greater equality between the French and Muslim populations in Algeria. They wanted to maintain Algeria as a French colony but address the inequalities that prevented Muslims from becoming French citizens. The second group, generally made up of younger Algerians, favored a far more dramatic change in Algeria. They wanted independence from France.

The failure of the Blum-Viollette bill to pass suggested to Muslims in both groups that they would never enjoy equal rights while Algeria remained a French colony. Gradually, more and more Muslims began to support the idea of independence, using violent means if necessary.

NATIONALISM ON THE RISE

In the years before, during, and after World War II, the more moderate groups within the Algerian Muslim community began to ally themselves with those who held more radical plans for the territory. Several men inspired the growing idea of an independent Algeria, and three emerged as key figures in the movement. One was Abd al-Hamid Ben Badis, a deeply conservative Islamic leader. Believing that Algeria had been corrupted by the presence of the French, he thought that only through independence could his country return to its Islamic roots.

Messali Hadj headed a more radical faction. Messali had come from a humble family and had little formal education. He had served in the French army and was married to a Frenchwoman. Through his brief membership in the Communist Party, he was influenced to call for a redistribution of land among the peasants. He was also one of the first native Algerians to call for revolution and for the seizure of all property belonging to the French government or the colons. He created several political parties, forming a new one when French authorities banned its earlier incarnation, including the Étoile Nord-Africaine (North African Star), the Parti Progressiste Algérien (Algerian Progressive Party), and the Mouvement pour le Triomphe des Libertés Démocratiques (Movement for the Triumph of Democratic Freedoms). Messali's outspoken positions frequently brought him into conflict with French authorities, who imprisoned him several times.

The third leading figure in the early nationalist movement was Ferhat Abbas, who was viewed as the most liberal of the three. Abbas's story demonstrates how the more moderate Muslims in Algeria gradually moved to a radical position. Abbas's father had been born into a poor peasant family but

In this circa-1946 photo, the Algerian political leader Ferhat Abbas is seen. Abbas initially believed Algerians would have greater rights as French citizens if the territory was annexed by France but later wanted Algeria to become an independent nation.

had risen up through the ranks to become a local political leader and a commander of the Legion of Honor. Abbas viewed his father's experience as proof that Muslims could succeed in the French colonial system. Abbas studied at a French school in Constantine and then became a pharmacist in Sétif. His first wife was Muslim, but he later divorced her and married a Frenchwoman.

In 1936, Abbas demonstrated his belief that it was possible, in fact necessary, for Muslims to be integrated into the French society. He declared:

> I will not die for the Algerian nation, because it does not exist. I have not found it. I have examined History, I questioned the living and the dead, I visited cemeteries; nobody spoke to me about it. I then turned to the Koran and I sought for one solitary verse forbidding a Muslim from integrating himself with a non-Muslim nation. I did not find that either.[5]

At the time, Abbas believed that the political actions in France were leading to greater rights for Muslims and that French citizenship would lead to a more vital, equal role for Muslims in their country. But the defeat of the Blum-Viollette proposal was a bitter disappointment to Algerian Muslims— and a sign to Abbas and many like him that the French would never accept them.

AFTER WORLD WAR II

The events of World War II provided additional sparks to the fiery spirit of nationalism that was growing in Algeria. After France was defeated by Nazi Germany in 1940, some in Algeria began to question the need to pay taxes to France when France itself was now no longer a fully independent nation. During the German occupation of France, food shortages and economic suffering in Algeria were rampant. Many Algerians who had fought for France in the war were injured or killed.

In November 1942, American forces landed in North Africa and quickly liberated Algeria. At the time, Algeria was operating under the control of France's Vichy government, which had been set up in France following its defeat. The Vichy government was the official government of France from July 1940 to August 1944, but in fact it was a puppet government heavily dependent on German goodwill. When American forces easily liberated Algeria from the Vichy government, the United States demonstrated the weakness of France to the Algerians.

They also exposed Algerians to the ideas proclaimed in the Atlantic Charter, the document signed in 1941 by the leaders of Great Britain and the United States—Prime Minister Winston Churchill and President Franklin Delano Roosevelt, respectively. A counterweight to the brutal ideology of Nazi Germany, the Atlantic Charter stated that people had the right to choose their own form of government. While Churchill apparently had stated that the charter was specific to Nazi-occupied Europe (to prevent British colonies from using the charter as a justification for independence), Algerians were quick to identify the ideals spelled out in the Atlantic Charter and claim that they should belong to all peoples, not simply those in Europe.

Ferhalt Abbas arranged a meeting with the American envoy in Algiers and explained how Algeria's treatment at the hands of France demonstrated a clear violation of the Atlantic Charter. Abbas noted that Algeria's continued participation in the war was dependent on the aims of the Allies. Was it truly, as Roosevelt had stated, a war of liberation for people, regardless of religion or race?

The envoy was sympathetic, prompting Abbas to draft a nine-page document of Algerian demands in February 1943. This document, the "Manifesto of the Algerian People," noted how France had routinely subjugated Algeria's Muslim population: "It is enough to examine the process of colonization in Algeria to realize how the policy of 'assimilation,' automatically applied to some and denied to others, has reduced Muslim society to utter servitude."[6] The manifesto also called for an end to colonialism, a guarantee of freedom and equality for all Algerians without regard to race or religion, and a redistribution of land held by wealthy colons to Arab peasants. In addition, it called for the establishment of Arabic and French as official languages, freedom of speech and association, free education for children of both sexes, a separation of church and state, the entry of Muslims into the Algerian government, and the release of political prisoners.

This manifesto demonstrated Abbas's growing disillusion with the willingness of the French to independently allow greater freedoms for Algerian citizens of all religious backgrounds. That said, the manifesto was also clearly a plan for Algeria to continue to remain part of French territory. Nowhere did it call for the creation of a new, independent nation.

The manifesto was handed to representatives of the Free French and Allied forces in Algeria on March 31, 1943. Nearly two months later, on May 26, Abbas produced an "Addition to the Manifesto," a response to a request from the governor-general for specific and concrete proposals to enact the demands made in the original document. This addition contained a highly significant paragraph, a sign that Abbas and his supporters now recognized that independence was the only way to achieve their aims:

> It is an established fact, proclaimed by French statesmen and jurists, that France, a Christian and Latin nation, cannot, without compromising her national unity, accept within her community and family an Algerian who does not abjure [reject] his faith. In these circumstances, it is only fair and human that an Algerian should at least be a citizen of his

own country. This is the clearest and simplest justification
for the recognition of the Algerian nation.[7]

A few weeks after the addition was made public, Abbas was
placed under house arrest. The struggle for Algerian independence was about to begin.

6

The Struggle for Freedom

While the Free French ignored the major demands of Ferhalt Abbas's manifesto, they did, in March 1944, agree to extend citizenship to a small number of Algerians— approximately 65,000. This token gesture proved unsatisfying to more militant Algerians, who were weary of French citizenship being doled out in tiny slivers to one group after another. Moderates also voiced their complaints. Among them was Abbas, who formally decided that same month to join forces with Messali Hadj in a new organization known as the Amis du Manifeste et de la Liberté (AML)—the Friends of the Manifesto and Liberty. The AML's stated goal was "to propagate the idea of an Algerian nation, and the desire for an Algerian constitution."[1] While the AML did not survive for very long, its formation was significant. It represented a unity among the different Muslim groups in Algeria and a determination to work toward a single purpose: the creation of an independent Algerian nation.

When World War II ended in 1945, France lost the prestige it had enjoyed as a global power. Although this was a tremendous change, particularly in the eyes of the Algerian nationalists, the French seemed determined to return to "business as usual" in Algeria. The French army was sent in to police the country; the colons were determined to preserve the status quo; and their representatives in the French government were ready do everything in their power to block any reforms.

It was this climate of suspicion and underlying anger that led to the previously described events in Sétif in 1945. After French police fired upon Muslims protesters, violence then spread through the countryside, targeting symbols of French administration and colons.

Word of the initial murder of 103 settlers at the hands of Muslim protesters, and the massacre of thousands of Muslims at the hands of the French in retaliation, sparked very different reactions, depending on the audience. For the French, the ability to put down a violent group of protesters was reassuring evidence that, after being occupied by a foreign power for several years, France was once more in command. But the experience also served to create a new and far larger group of nationalists in Algeria. The writer Kateb Yacine, a 16-year-old when the fierce repression began in Algeria, looked back on the events at Sétif as personally transforming: "The shock which I felt at the pitiless butchery that caused the deaths of thousands of Muslims, I have never forgotten. From that moment my nationalism took definite form."[2] For Algerian soldiers who were returning after fighting for France in the war, the news that French soldiers had murdered their countrymen was almost inconceivable.

On August 27, 1947, the French government once again attempted to appease the nationalists through legal reform.

This special statute for Algeria included an acceptance of Arabic as well as French as an official language in Algeria. It included a policy that extended the vote to Muslim women, who previously had been excluded from voting. It also created an elected assembly for Algeria that would vote on a budget and finance laws and have some power to modify local laws. But the French also took steps to prevent representatives from the more militant political parties from being elected to the Algerian Assembly, and many of the more important reforms were never implemented. The Algerian Assembly proved short-lived; it was dissolved in April 1956.

L'ORGANISATION SPÉCIALE

The most militant and fiery Algerians began to join a new paramilitary group, L'Organisation spéciale (OS), or Special Organization. The OS had been formed covertly in 1947; most of its members were young men in their twenties from middle-class backgrounds. One of these young revolutionaries was Ahmed Ben Bella.

Ben Bella, as a young man, had been a promising soccer player. He joined the French army, rising to the rank of sergeant major, and received awards for his service. After serving in World War II, he returned to Algeria and was horrified at the stories of the massacre at Sétif. He came to the conclusion that the only possible solution to the injustice and unrest was an independent Algeria, governed by Algerians. Ben Bella then resigned his military commission and briefly considered a career in politics before deciding to immerse himself in the revolutionary cause. Like many young men of his age who played a critical role in the revolution, his wartime service provided him with a knowledge of military tactics that would aid him in the struggle for independence.

Hocine Aït Ahmed and Mohamed Boudiaf, both skilled fighters and passionate revolutionaries, joined Ben Bella in the OS. (Their importance in the struggle for independence would

Ahmed Ben Bella, who had served in the French army, became one of the leading Algerian revolutionaries during the Algerian War. After independence, he became the first president of Algeria, serving from 1963 to 1965.

be reflected in their postrevolution careers. Ben Bella would become the first post-independence president of Algeria, and Boudiaf the fourth. Aït Ahmed would become a key figure in the political opposition.) The OS secretly trained an army of guerrilla fighters, a total of some 4,500 men, who began launching a campaign of terror in 1949. The first target was the central post office in Oran. Attacks on other symbols of French power followed.

The French were aware of the OS and did their best to infiltrate the organization and track its activities. By the spring of 1950, members of the OS began to be arrested, and within a year many of its members fled or were captured and arrested. The French also located many of the stores of weapons that the OS had hidden. Ben Bella himself was captured, although he was able to escape to Egypt.

Ben Bella was eventually able to rally the OS members who had been able to escape. He, Aït Ahmed, Boudiaf, and several others formed the core of a new organization in 1954, one intended not to launch terrorist attacks but instead to prepare the country for an armed struggle for independence. This new organization was called the Comité Révolutionnaire pour l'Unité et l'Action (Revolutionary Committee for Unity and Action). This group met secretly both in Algiers and in Switzerland. Its members began to plan the almost overwhelming task of ending the rule of a country that had occupied their land for more than 100 years.

In October 1954, the Revolutionary Committee—ready to move from the planning phase to a time of action—renamed and reorganized itself. There were now two wings of the same group: the political wing, the Front de Libération Nationale (FLN), and the military wing, the Armée de Libération Nationale (ALN)—although the actions of the two wings were generally attributed to the FLN. Ben Bella and his fellow members put their military training into practice, dividing Algeria into six administrative areas, or *wilayas*. A seventh was later added—mainland France. The ALN organized its fighters into companies of 100 men and sections of 30 men, copying the French military structure.[3]

The goal of what followed was to create a climate of insecurity and violence so constant that the French would have to respond in as public a way as possible, which would bring Algeria's struggle to the attention of the world. The leaders of the FLN recognized that France had an overwhelming advantage militarily. It had more soldiers, who were far better equipped. But the FLN believed that, once Algeria's struggle drew enough international attention, international pressure would force France to decolonize Algeria.

On November 1, 1954, All Saints' Day (a religious holiday in France and French territory), the FLN launched its attack at several different spots around Algeria. The FLN had fairly small numbers and lacked a large cache of weapons, and it concentrated much of its efforts in the Aurès Mountains. The purpose of several smaller attacks in other parts of the country was to suggest that their numbers were widespread and that they had far greater resources than they actually did.

At 1:00 A.M., a group of FLN members entered the town of Batna, headed for the military barracks there, and killed the two sentries on guard. At 3:00 A.M., there was an attack on the military garrison in Khenchela, east of Batna; gunfire was exchanged, and a French lieutenant was fatally wounded. At 7:00 A.M., a third group ambushed a bus passing through the Tighanimine gorges. The FLN had learned that a local political figure who was loyal to the French was traveling on that bus. His destination was the town of Arris, where he was to warn French authorities that a revolt was brewing. He was found on the bus and ordered off, along with a young couple—French teachers who were newlyweds. The three were then shot. Some reports suggest that the political figure reached for a gun first and that the teachers were accidently shot during the exchange of fire. The body of the local politician was taken to Arris and

ANTICOLONIALISM

Ahmed Ben Bella and the other members of the Revolutionary Committee were encouraged by anticolonial sentiment that was growing not only in Algeria but also throughout much of the world. In the years after World War II, many European powers found themselves in the position of allowing their colonies to win their independence. This was not due to a sudden desire on the part of European nations to spread freedom throughout the globe, but instead was a result of similar factors to those experienced in Algeria. The long years of war had been costly for many Allied nations; indeed, economies all over the world struggled to recover in the postwar era. The citizens of such world powers as Great Britain were no longer willing to pay for maintaining an empire in distant lands when basic staples of life were so scarce at home. (India, for example, achieved its independence from Britain in 1947, and a new Muslim nation—Pakistan—was carved out of part of what had once been British India.) Abroad, the people in those colonies—many of whom had fought during the war to help protect the freedom of people in Europe—now questioned why those same rights to self-determination and independence did not extend to them.

Much of the modern Middle East began to take shape in the years after World War II. A desire for unity brought together several of the Arab nations in the Arab League, which was formed in 1945. Its members included Egypt, Iraq, Lebanon, Saudi Arabia, Syria, Jordan (known then as Transjordan), and Yemen. Perhaps most significant to the people of Algeria was a growing nationalist movement in the neighboring French colonies of Morocco and Tunisia, and the defeat of the French in 1954 in their efforts to retain their colony of Indochina (known today as Vietnam).

The Algerian War began on November 1, 1954, when FLN guerrillas attacked military and civilian targets across Algeria. Seen here, House Bouchemal, where the uprising in the Aurès Mountains started.

left there as a sign to others to cooperate with the FLN and resist the French authorities. The teachers were left on the side of the road, where they bled to death.

Shortly after the attacks, a message to the Algerian people from the FLN was broadcast on Radio Cairo:

A group of responsible young people and dedicated militants, gathering about it the majority of wholesome and resolute elements, has judged that the moment has come to take the National Movement out of the impasse into which it has been forced by the conflicts of person and influence, and to launch it into the true revolutionary struggle at the side of the Moroccan and Tunisian brothers. . . .[4]

The message then invited all Algerians to join in the "national struggle." It stated that the revolution's goals were national independence through "restoration of the Algerian state, sovereign, democratic, and social, within the framework of the principles of Islam" and "preservation of all fundamental freedoms, without distinction of race or religion."[5] French people living in Algeria had a choice, according to the message: They could retain their own nationality, in which case they would be considered foreigners, or they could become Algerian citizens.

The war for Algerian independence began with those scattered attacks on November 1, 1954. A local politician and two newlywed French teachers were the first victims. At the time, few on either side of the conflict could imagine that the war would last for eight years. Nearly one million European settlers would be forced from their homes, and an estimated one million Muslim Algerians would lose their lives before it came to an end.

A Time of War

The attacks on All Saints' Day sparked outrage in the colon community. Colons turned to French authorities and demanded an end to any talk of reforms or greater voting rights until order had been restored. In France, the response was more muted. The attacks fell under the jurisdiction of the Interior Ministry, which is responsible for the internal security of France, civil defense, and law enforcement, among many other responsibilities.

At the time, the minister of the interior was François Mitterrand, who would later serve as French president from 1981 to 1995. Mitterrand had been an opponent of the efforts to push for greater reforms in Algeria. Shortly after the attacks, he spoke in the French Assembly about the matter, declaring, "Algeria is France. And who among you, *Mesdames, Messieurs*, would hesitate to employ every means to preserve France?"[1]

The French government was in a difficult position. Officials were unwilling to negotiate directly with the leaders of the FLN who had participated in the attacks, but there was no other Algerian leader with whom they could negotiate to bring an end to the conflict. The colon community was a powerful voting lobby that threatened to vote out government officials who did not move swiftly and forcefully to restore order. The French were not even sure who precisely was in the FLN, meaning they did not know who was responsible for the attacks. They arrested several of the "usual suspects," thus adding to the militants many young men who had been falsely accused and imprisoned in this roundup.

The French army was dispatched to the sites of the attacks, but the mountainous region was difficult for cumbersome tanks and troop transports to navigate. The military officials in charge of the region had little or no experience with guerrilla warfare, nor did their troops. Arriving in winter, the soldiers were cold and poorly supplied. One French soldier noted his shock at arriving in the inhospitable and icy region of Khenchela and seeing the starving people living "merely on stones and air" while the wealthy colons protested, "They don't have the same needs as us!"[2]

The French distributed fliers to the local population, warning against any cooperation with the rebels and urging them to come down from their homes in the hills and relocate to a safer location. The fliers included a warning that "a terrifying calamity" would soon be unleashed upon the rebels and any who cooperated with them. But the few who came down from the hills were mostly women and children, and no "terrifying calamity" followed, encouraging a belief that French threats— like their promises—were generally empty.

The Algerian war for independence carried an unusual set of circumstances. Generally, a war for independence is fought between two groups—the colonial power and the native people. But in this war, the situation was further complicated by a third

During the Algerian War, military operations were conducted along the Algerian-Tunisian border, where French troops put up barbed-wire fences to prevent supplies from being ferreted over the border to Algerian fighters. Seen here, French troops patrol the Laverdure area in June 1958.

group—the descendants of the settlers who first arrived from Europe and were Algerian by birth. This group often reacted with force to any attempt on the part of the French government to appease or negotiate with the Algerian rebels.

The French were able to inflict some early losses on the rebels, but the rebels became increasingly well armed. While their suppliers remain unknown, many reports have suggested that the rebels received armaments from Libya. When Tunisia and Morocco won their independence in March 1956, men and supplies (including weapons) could easily move in and out of Algeria from those neighboring countries. Because the Algerian independence movement had strong support in those two countries, the French constructed a series of barbed-wire fences and observation posts along Algeria's borders with Morocco and Tunisia. The fence that separated Morocco from Algeria was more than 621 miles (1,000 kilometers) long; traces of it still exist today. The so-called Morice Line stretched for 200 miles (322 kilometers) along the border that separated Algeria and Tunisia. It was charged with electric volts, and mines were planted in the fields along the fence.

The rebels faced not only attacks from the French army but also from vigilante groups formed by the colons in more remote farming regions. Launching what they called *raton-nades*—"rat hunts"—they roamed the countryside looking for anyone they suspected of rebel activity and brutally murdering them, actions that met with little or no reaction from France. Soon the countryside became so unsafe and violent that thousands of colons began to flee Algiers, heading for France.

FIGHTING IN THE STREETS

By 1957, the FLN could boast of more than 40,000 guerrillas fighting for Algerian independence. Its tactics relied on night raids and ambushes on civilian and military targets. In the spring of 1957 alone, the FLN carried out more than 800 attacks. Its presence was strongest in the Massif de l'Aurès, the Kabylier, and the mountains surrounding Algiers, Constantine, and Oran, but it increasingly launched attacks in the streets of Algiers as well. There was also heavy fighting along Algeria's borders with Morocco and Tunisia, where rebel Algerians sought to break through the borders and restore free traffic with those neighboring countries.

Even with these successes, the fighting seemed to be shifting in France's favor by the spring of 1958. Fewer rebel attacks were launched in the cities and in the countryside, and efforts to break through the barriers along the border had failed. Yet, the French government was under its own pressures. The cost of fighting a war in Algeria—in terms of defense spending and human lives—was growing, as was French public opinion opposed to the war. Nearly half a million men were stationed in Algeria, many of whom had been drafted. Some returned home with stories of the horrible economic divisions that kept Muslim Algeria in poverty. Many veterans also told stories of suspects brutally tortured in order to extract information. And then there was the scorched-earth policy employed by the French forces. Families and even entire villages suspected of aiding the FLN were subjected to collective punishment. Homes were burned and farmlands destroyed.

In April 1958, at the moment that a new government was being formed in France (similar to a transition of power after an election in the United States), it seemed likely that this new government would be more moderate and willing to negotiate a settlement with the rebels to bring an end to the war. The colons were furious. The trigger proved to be an act of retaliation. The French had arrested and executed three men charged with terrorism, and the FLN responded by executing three French prisoners.

The colon community decided to take matters into its own hands. On May 13, a mob gathered at a war monument in a park in Algiers just below the palace that housed the governor-general. The colors then proclaimed the formation of the Committee of Safety. Mobs rushed into the governor-general's headquarters and other key French government offices. It was a coup that threatened the French government, which now found itself under attack from both the rebels and the colons. This attack would serve to bring down the newly formed government.

ENTER DE GAULLE

The government of the Fourth Republic, overwhelmed by the French losses in Indochina and its inability to resolve the Algerian crisis, collapsed in May 1958. In September of the same year, a referendum was held in France in which nearly

80 percent of those who voted supported the creation of a new constitution and a new government, the Fifth Republic. In this political vacuum, there was an immediate need for a strong leader to take charge, reassure the French people, provide forceful leadership for the government, and bring order

CHARLES DE GAULLE

Charles André Joseph Marie de Gaulle was born in 1890 and grew up in Paris, the son of a teacher. He chose a military career and served with distinction in World War I. In the 1930s, he argued for a stronger military defense against Germany. When Germany defeated France in May 1940, he was serving as under-secretary of defense and war. De Gaulle refused to accept the peace treaty France signed with Germany and instead escaped to London. There he announced the formation of the French government in exile, which became known as the "Free French." He became a powerful symbol of the French struggle against German occupation. When France was liberated in 1944, he received a hero's welcome in Paris. He became president of the provisional government in France immediately after liberation. But in 1946, after his efforts to strengthen the power of the presidency were blocked, he resigned.

In the immediate postwar era, de Gaulle remained a very popular figure. His reputation for strength and his heroic status within the French army made him the best choice to lead the new French government, the Fifth Republic, the constitution of which was ratified in September 1958. As part of de Gaulle's conditions for accepting the job, the constitution of the Fifth Republic greatly strengthened the powers of France's executive branch.

in Algeria. In November 1958, elections were held in France to appoint a new and more stable government. The man chosen to lead it was Charles de Gaulle, the former general who had led the Free French Forces during World War II.

In the run-up to the November election, de Gaulle flew to Algeria on June 4, 1958. (Just a few days earlier, he had become prime minister and been granted emergency powers for six months by the National Assembly.) He spent three days touring the country. He gave an emotional speech in Algiers, in which he raised his arms and called out, "*Je vous ai compris!*" ("I have understood you!"). In his speech, he reassured his audience that all of the inhabitants of Algeria were Frenchmen and offered a promise of reconciliation, in particular with the "Muslim Frenchmen."[3]

Within a few months, de Gaulle proposed a series of policies designed to move Algeria in the direction he had outlined during his speech. He proposed steps to give the right to vote to all Algerians, male and female, and to guarantee that at least two-thirds of Algeria's representatives to the legislature of the Fifth Republic were Muslim. In the so-called Constantine Plan of October 1958, he offered a five-year program in which education would be expanded; 618,000 acres (250,000 hectares) of French-held lands would be redistributed; and industrial investment would increase, with the goal of adding 400,000 new jobs.

The focus of de Gaulle's efforts was to integrate Algeria back into France. Not surprisingly, this brought him into conflict with the leaders of the FLN, whose goal was an independent Algeria. Their first test was an election held in Algeria to vote on the reforms. The FLN called for a boycott of the elections. But now equipped with the right to vote, some for the first time in their lives, nearly 80 percent of Muslim men and women showed up to vote, and 96 percent voted to approve the Fifth Republic's constitution.[4]

The FLN responded by launching a series of terrorist attacks in France itself, while at the same time reaching out

The Algerian crisis helped return General Charles de Gaulle to power. He is seen here in Mostaganem, Algeria, in June 1958, uttering the famous phrase "Long live French Algeria" during a speech in which he examined the colony's future without giving any specifics to his imminent plans.

diplomatically to leaders of friendly nations. The second part of this response was particularly effective because it increased the flow of military supplies to the FLN and even led to a diplomatic meeting in China. On September 19, 1958, at a press conference held in Cairo, Egypt, the FLN announced the formation of a provisional government, the Gouvernement Provisoire de la République Algérienne (GPRA). Its president was Ferhat Abbas, who was chosen in part for his more moderate image inside and outside Algeria; Ahmed Ben Bella was named vice president. The capital was in Tunis, in the nation of Tunisia.

A WAR IN TWO PARTS

Historians of the Algerian Revolution speak of it as a war in two parts. The first part, from November 1954 to September 1958, focused on converting the Algerian people to the idea of revolution and working inside Algeria to prepare the country to fight for independence. The second phase, from late 1958 until 1962, when independence was achieved, focused more on activities outside Algeria—on diplomatic and political actions designed to rally international support for Algeria's independence movement. As representatives of the provisional government began to travel to foreign capitals, where they were treated with courtesy and, in some cases, as official diplomats, the FLN's prestige and power began to grow.

With this, a shift began to become clear in de Gaulle's efforts to move toward integrating Algeria into France. Elections held in November 1958, intended to select Algeria's deputies to the first legislature of the Fifth Republic, saw a much lower voter turnout, and no Muslim of political stature chose to run.

Threats began to mass along the borders, as external branches of the ALN (the military wing of the FLN) began to form in neighboring countries. These external ALN armies were formed from ALN members who had fled across the border, as well as from civilian refugees and willing volunteers from such countries as Morocco and Tunisia. Because they were not under constant attack (as units in Algeria were), these external units could develop orderly systems for recruiting, training, and developing strategy. Also, weapons and supplies reached them more easily.

International pressure began to increase on the French, as did internal pressure. Popular support for the war was steadily falling in mainland France, as the years passed and no solution seemed achievable. Realizing he needed to address the problem, de Gaulle gave a televised speech in France on September 16, 1959. For the first time, he offered a new compromise to the Algerian question—"self-determination." Once peace had been restored in Algeria, its people would have the right to choose their own destiny: association with France, integration into France, or independence.

The speech was well received by its intended audience, the people of mainland France, but its effect in Algeria was electrifying and divisive. To many Algerian Muslims, it demonstrated that even the French government was now recognizing that independence might be a possibility, giving tremendous support to the revolutionary movement. To the soldiers of the French army, however, the speech made them question why they were being asked to fight and die to hold onto a territory that the French government might ultimately decide to give up. In the colon community, this speech was clear evidence that the French government was no longer willing to protect its interests and its land.

By November 1959, the colons had formed what they called the Front National Français to protect and defend their rights. They raised barricades in the city and fired on local law enforcement officials while the French army watched and did not interfere. After some effort, de Gaulle was able to restore order and have the barricades removed. But for the remaining years of the war, the protests of the colons and the anger from the military would add to the tensions that helped to prevent France from recognizing the inevitability of Algerian independence.

The Final Struggle

The final years of the Algerian struggle for independence were brutal. One of the most famous voices during this period was that of Frantz Fanon, who is often described as the "prophet of the Algerian revolution."[1] Born in 1925, Fanon was not Algerian by birth, but instead was born in the French territory of Martinique in the Caribbean.

Like Ahmed Ben Bella, Fanon had served in Italy as part of the Free French campaign during World War II. After the war, he became a practicing psychiatrist. His first book, *Black Skins, White Masks*, published in 1952, was a critique of French racism. It presented Fanon's belief that French Caribbeans like himself would never be truly French citizens because their skin color prevented them from achieving true acceptance into French society.

In October 1953, Fanon began working at a hospital south of Algiers. As the hospital's psychiatrist, Fanon was overwhelmed

The revolutionary French psychiatrist, social philosopher, and author Frantz Fanon was a firm supporter of the Algerian struggle for independence and became a member of the Algerian National Liberation Front. In the years since his death in 1961, his writings have inspired numerous anticolonial liberation movements.

by the number of Algerians suffering from mental-health issues. In his view, this epidemic was a direct result of French colonialism because French rule had made these people feel unworthy and inferior. By 1956, he had decided to leave the hospital and join the FLN in Tunisia, where he began writing reports for the FLN newspaper, *El Moudjahid*. In 1959, he published a nonfiction work on the crisis, *L'An Cinq de la Révolution Algérienne (Year Five of the Algerian Revolution)*. Published in Paris, the book was immediately banned. Fanon's argument was that the Algeria that was emerging during the struggle—the Algeria that must become independent—was not the Algeria that had existed before the French invasion in 1830. Instead it was a new, idealized Algeria, one in which, for example, the young women who were carrying weapons would no longer be content with subservient roles or to be hidden away.

Fanon's most famous, and most militant, work was *Les Damnés de la Terre (The Wretched of the Earth)*. It was published in 1961, shortly before his death from leukemia. In this work, Fanon expressed his belief that, as in Algeria, the downtrodden and poor would be the leaders of a revolution in the Third World, creating societies free from the imperialism and fascism that marked European societies. In this work, Fanon even offered a defense of the violence that accompanied revolution, explaining that it was a necessary counterpart to the racism and violent suppression that marked colonial rule. Only by demonstrating their willingness to use violence to achieve their aims, Fanon believed, could former colonies rid themselves of the lingering inferiority and subservience that had marked their oppression by a foreign power. Through Fanon's writings, the revolution in Algeria would become an important symbol for radical movements in the 1960s, including the Black Panthers in the United States and French students who launched protests in Paris in 1968.

The violence Fanon had written of became clear in the final months of the Algerian War. The colons had joined forces with certain disaffected members of the French military to form a group called the Organisation de l'Armée Secrète (OAS)—the Organization of the Secret Army. Convinced that President de Gaulle was preparing to give away their country, the OAS unleashed hit squads that roamed the streets, targeting Muslims, liberals willing to compromise, settlers preparing to leave Algeria, and even units of the French army. Corpses were regularly discovered on the main streets of Algiers; in fact, the OAS murdered 230 Muslims in Algiers during the first week of May 1962 alone.[2] The OAS also set fire to the library at the University of Algiers, torched oil refineries, and dynamited the town hall in Oran.

The FLN met this violence with violence. OAS bars were targeted, vacated property was seized, and settlers were subjected to attacks and torture. By April 1962, approximately 100,000 settlers and their descendants had fled Algeria; by August, this number had grown to almost one million, nearly the entire colon population.[3]

CEASEFIRE

After many officials in France vowed that the government would never negotiate with the FLN, it did just that when it began talks with FLN representatives in Evian, France, in May 1961. During the negotiations, the French representatives argued for protection for the French minority that was expected to remain in Algeria, including the right to dual citizenship, normal civil and political rights, and rights to their property. French representatives also fought for retained control of the Sahara, where major oil deposits had been found in 1956, and for the right to maintain French military bases on Algerian soil. The Algerian response was that such arrangements could only be made once Algeria was independent and thus capable of negotiating on an equal footing with France.

The negotiations continued, off and on, for nearly a year. Finally, an agreement was reached and a 93-page document

Seen here, people gather in 1962 to celebrate Algerian independence. Though the long struggle for independence was over, the making of a nation was just beginning.

was signed at Evian on March 18, 1962. The document began with a formal recognition of the independence of the entire territory of Algeria. It also called for an immediate ceasefire, to go into effect the following day. The ceasefire, however, did not bring an end to the violence. In fact, the OAS responded to it with even more violent and bloody attacks.

Though it had lost its colony, France did not leave the negotiations empty-handed. The agreement provided France with leases on its air and naval facilities in Algeria, as well as a guarantee of all oil exploration and production rights already in existence with French companies and preferential treatment for French firms in any new contracts awarded in the next six years. At the same time, it granted Algeria ownership of its own oil reserves.

France's biggest loss, apart from losing its colony, was its inability to protect its Algerian-born citizens. As previously mentioned, the majority of colons chose to leave Algeria once it was clear that independence would become a reality. In the final months, a number of colons destroyed libraries, hospitals, government buildings, factories, and machinery—a last vindictive act in the country that many of them had called home for four or five generations.[4]

On July 1, 1962, a referendum was held in Algeria. In that election, the people of Algeria voted 5,975,581 to 16,534 in favor of independence.[5] On July 3, at 10:30 A.M., Charles de Gaulle announced that Algeria was an independent nation. In Algeria, the news was met with widespread celebration; in France, feelings were far more mixed, especially when one considers how much the French nation had lost in blood, treasure, and international prestige. During the eight years of the Algerian conflict, approximately 18,000 French soldiers and 10,000 European settlers had been killed, as had one million Muslim Algerians (70,000 of these by the FLN).[6]

After
the Revolution

One hundred and thirty-two years after the flag of the French king had first been flown over the Qasba in Algiers, Algeria achieved its independence. But the new nation faced serious challenges that would endure into the early twenty-first century.

After the majority of the European Algerians had left Algeria, groups acted out their frustration and disappointment by destroying schools, libraries, hospitals, factories, and other key pieces of the former colony's infrastructure. Additionally, since many of these people had occupied important roles in Algeria's professional, technical, and governmental services, their loss was keenly felt. Moreover, in addition to losing these people's expertise, Algeria lost its wealth; the money that had been spent employing local workers and purchasing local goods was gone. In the first years of independence, Algeria's economy suffered in this vacuum. Today, it is estimated that up to 70 percent of Algeria's male workers were unemployed or underemployed in 1963.[1]

This economic crisis called for a swift government response that would impose controls, create jobs, and provide the training and infrastructure the new country desperately needed after years of war. The leaders of the FLN, however, were not economists or political scientists by training; they were revolutionaries. Once the war had ended, many of them had begun focusing on increasing their political power.

Once the FLN members had brought independence to Algeria, some of the differences that had originally made it difficult for them to come together again surfaced. Some believed that independence was only the beginning of the revolution, that it marked the first step in a dramatic transformation of Algerian society. For others, independence was the end of the revolution, and now attention needed to be turned toward reestablishing the same structures that had governed colonial life.

In late 1963, Ahmed Ben Bella became Algeria's first elected president. The economic, social, and political challenges the new country faced were overwhelming. Ben Bella's efforts—in addition to consolidating his own power—involved developing socialist programs. These included nationalizing all properties vacated by the departing Europeans, as well as the farms belonging to colons, and turning them into collectives to be run by local groups.

His efforts to increase his hold on power, however, soon began to alienate friends and the people he was trying to govern. A former teammate of Ben Bella's from school said, after his election as president, that he had been "a good soccer player, but he never forgot the galleries. He wanted to be number one. Ben Bella always wanted his teammates to pass him the ball so that he could score. He was the same way in politics."[2]

Among the alienated was Ferhat Abbas, who, after criticizing some of Ben Bella's anti-Western policies, was forced out of the FLN in 1963. Mohamed Boudiaf, another of the men who had helped form the revolutionary movement, was arrested on Ben Bella's orders. A number of the president's other former revolutionary comrades were forced out of office, imprisoned, moved into exile, or in the case of at least one, Hocine Aït Ahmed, mysteriously assassinated.

Scandals and corruption soon overwhelmed Ben Bella's administration at the same time that nearly 2 million Algerians were unemployed. In 1964, the president's residence was attacked and riots broke out; by 1965, the military was threatening a coup. On June 19, 1965, Algerians heard a message broadcast on Radio Algiers at noon. The message, from a group calling itself the Council of the Revolution, informed Algerians that the army had seized power because, after three years of independence, the government had been crippled by "sordid calculations, political narcissism, and the morbid love of power." The council promised to organize "a democratic and responsible state ordered by laws and founded in morality, a state capable of outliving governments and individuals."[3] Ben Bella was forced out of office and arrested; he would remain in prison for the next 14 years. The new leader of Algeria was its defense secretary, Colonel Houari Boumedienne.

COLONEL BOUMEDIENNE

Although Boumedienne had served in the FLN with Ben Bella as chief of staff, he had very different views about how Algeria should be run. (Despite the differences between the two men, the FLN remained the only political party in Algeria during Boumedienne's administration.) His immediate focus was on rebuilding Algeria's economy and correcting the skyrocketing unemployment that had forced many Algerians to seek work in France, where they faced discrimination and prejudice.

The discovery of oil and gas reserves in the Sahara provided a boost to Algeria's economy, but the wealth from this discovery did not trickle down to ordinary Algerians. Therefore,

Houari Boumedienne served as president of Algeria from 1965 to his death in December 1978. During his presidency, he sought to create a national identiy for Algerians and promote greater economic opportunities for Algerians, but he also consolidated considerable power in his own office.

Boumedienne's goal was to transform Algeria into a well-rounded industrialized nation. Now that the revolution had created the nation of Algeria, Boumedienne recognized the need to create an Algerian national identity. It was clear there were several ways to create a sense of national unity. Although Boumedienne's view was that the Islamic religion should not dictate government policy, he established a policy of state control of religion in which religious leaders were subject to the regulations of the Algerian Ministry of Religious Affairs.

In addition to controlling religion, Boumedienne used education and military service as ways to create a national identity. Education would help transform Algeria into a modern country; military service would help foster pride in the nation. In fact, Boumedienne encouraged the creation of a kind of myth about the Algerian army. Monuments were erected and memorials were organized to celebrate the role played by the army in leading a revolution "by the people and for the people."[4] The grim and often violent reality of the years of revolution was gradually whitewashed by this emerging mythology, in which the members of the Algerian military were transformed into the heroic protectors of the revolution.

Language was another focus of control for the Boumedienne regime. Arabic was adopted as the official language in Algeria. When a proposal was made to elevate the Berber language to equal status with Arabic, government leaders denounced the plan as a path that might eventually lead to a separatist movement by Berbers. It was, however, much more difficult to eliminate French from daily use. In the years of French colonization, Algerians had become accustomed to using French for official communication; even after independence, many Algerians continued to immigrate to France for work. As late as the early 1970s, two Algerians meeting in the street were still most likely to greet each other in French.[5]

Under Boumedienne, the government took control of many industries, including minerals, banking, insurance, and manufacturing. In 1969, Algeria joined the Organization of Petroleum Exporting Countries (OPEC). The oil and gas industries were nationalized in February 1971. The rapid industrialization was intended in part to create jobs, but the jobs that were created were typically found in the cities along the Mediterranean coastline, not in the Algerian interior. Soon, more and more young Algerians were leaving farms and rural settings to move into the cities seeking work, resulting in civic overcrowding and a strain on urban resources. Slums began to appear around the cities of Algiers and Oran. Unemployment was at 22 percent in 1977, at a time when the population was exploding. The high birthrate placed a greater strain on schools and made it even more difficult for young Algerians to find work.

Boumedienne also oversaw the creation of a new constitution, known as the National Charter. Ratified in 1976, it guaranteed freedom of expression and assembly and provided protections for private property. The rights of women to participate in every aspect of national life were guaranteed. Islam was affirmed as the state religion. Gambling was outlawed, and the concept of the Muslim weekend (in which Friday is the day for attending worship services) was introduced. The charter also gave substantial powers to the president, who could be nominated by the FLN and then elected by popular vote for five-year terms. He could be reelected indefinitely. The president had the right to name his own cabinet. He could also appoint a prime minister or vice president, but he was not required to do so and could fire either of them whenever he chose. The president would also serve as commander in chief of the military and secretary-general of the FLN, Algeria's only official political party.

Boumedienne led Algeria for 13 years. Then, in 1978, he began appearing ill in public. Questions about his health were brushed aside; instead, public statements emphasized the strong role he was playing in international politics as he traveled more and more frequently abroad. Gradually, Algerians realized that Boumedienne was leaving the country so often because he was receiving medical treatment at foreign hospitals. In October, he left Algeria for Moscow, in what was then the Soviet Union. When he returned a few weeks later, he fell into a coma. (It was later revealed that he was suffering from a rare blood disease.) The government continued to issue reports of his vigor until his death on December 27, 1978, at the age of 53.

In later years, Boumedienne would be eulogized as a wise president whose focus was on protecting ordinary Algerians and as an honest leader who oversaw a strong economy and a unified nation. This nostalgia for the Algeria of the 1970s forgets that the economy was fragile and that Boumedienne's regime was marked by repression of his enemies and a lack of political freedom.

BLACK OCTOBER

Under the National Charter drafted under Boumedienne's leadership, the president of Algeria was nominated by the FLN, and so upon his death the FLN met in Algiers and nominated Colonel Chadli Bendjedid. Bendjedid had been a respected senior officer in the FLN's military wing, and his support from the military helped ensure his election.

Bendjedid had been born in 1929 to a family of farmers living in northeastern Algeria. He had been part of the resistance in 1955 and an officer among the external ALN forces based in Tunisia. He had been a loyal supporter of Boumedienne, but the country he inherited upon Boumedienne's death was filled with increasingly discontented people. The reasons for this discontent were as widespread as they were varied. University students were frustrated at the lack of job opportunities that awaited them after graduation and at the rapid increase in prices for books and other school supplies. A climate of uncertainty affected the economy, and people were frightened by rumors of pending mass layoffs and rumors of food and water shortages. At the same time, Islamists increasingly began to protest what they saw as a decline in standards of basic morality and decency, and assaults on what they called "traditional values." The government attempted to appease these groups by opening new mosques, but the protests continued.

On October 5, 1988, rioters and protesters spread through the streets of Algiers. Banners proclaiming "We are men!" and "We want our rights!" were held as crowds attacked department stores, cafés, restaurants, and government offices. Cars and trucks were overturned and set on fire. The violence spread out from the city over the next two days. In Blida (southwest of Algiers), the court buildings were set on fire and protesters filled the center of town. In Oran, two hotels were trashed and looted. The crowds, mostly young men dressed in jeans and sneakers, roamed the streets brandishing clubs and machetes.

President Bendjedid was criticized and laughed at by the protesters, who described him as dishonorable and dishonest and even an assassin. Stones and explosive devices were thrown in central Algiers, until the military announced that all civilian authorities were now under military command. Demonstrations were banned, a curfew was imposed in Algiers, and tanks moved into the streets of the capital. The army was given the right to shoot at any crowds that gathered; protesters could be arrested and tortured. Thousands of rioters were quickly rounded up and imprisoned. When scattered army units opened fire on protesters, popular anger intensified.

The third day of the crisis was a Friday. After the Friday prayers, 8,000 Islamic sympathizers took to the streets, where they confronted police and shouted "Islamic republic" and "Chadli murderer."[6] On October 10, an Islamist preacher organized a march of 20,000 people, who marched through the streets of Algiers to the sea, where a military barricade had been erected. For half an hour, there was a tense standoff. Reports differ about precisely what happened then—some say that a demonstrator fired on the army, while other reports claim that others hoping to spark a conflict fired gunshots. Whatever the triggering event, the result was that the army began firing into the crowd of marchers, killing 50 people.

When President Bendjedid went on television, he announced his intention to introduce political reforms that ultimately ended the FLN's control over Algeria. In November 1988, Algerians overwhelmingly supported a referendum to introduce a multiparty political system. The crisis that would become known as "Black October" had ended, but the country would not be the same. The army, which had been described as the guardian of Algeria, had fired upon its people. That event marked a dramatic division between the people of Algeria and their government.

REFORM AND CHANGE

Changes in the political system brought multiparty elections. The FLN was no longer guaranteed electoral victory simply because it was the only game in town. Instead, the Front Islamique du Salut (FIS)—the Islamic Salvation Front—quickly won the first round of multiparty elections held in Algeria. Algerian society was becoming increasingly polarized. Those supporting a more Islamic influence in Algeria came into conflict with Berbers and the supporters of women's rights. There were struggles among supporters of Berber culture, Arab culture, and French culture. Pro-Western idealists argued with pro-Arab idealists. And most people protested attempts by the military to regain its old influence.

In this political milieu, a leader of the FIS, Abbas Madani, made a fateful speech on November 1, 1990, warning of any attempt by the government to take back control: "By dialogue, we will change the regime. If it hangs back, then it will be jihad. . . . Algerians, your position is crucial. . . . This year will see the establishment of a Divine Republic."[7]

The government and military clearly recognized this provocative speech as a threat. The army chose to step in, dissolve the parliament, and force President Bendjedid to step down. The second round of elections was canceled, Madani was arrested, and other members of the FIS fled the country. Instead of a president, a five-man executive council—the Haut Conseil d'Etat (HCE)—was appointed to head the government; it was led by former revolutionary figure Mohamed Boudiaf. But Boudiaf's time in power was short; within six months, he was assassinated during a public ceremony marking the opening of a cultural center. Official reports said that a lone gunman, motivated by religious extremism, killed Boudiaf, but it seems unlikely that a lone gunman would have been able to kill the country's leader as well as wounding 40 members of the audience before escaping the guards who were there for the event.

Algeria soon found itself on the brink of a civil war. This war, labeled as a "Second War of Liberation," was launched by Islamic militants, many of whom were angry, unemployed young Algerians who welcomed the idea of a campaign of urban terrorism. There was not, however, a single organization directing their activities; instead, there were several different groups, each with its own leaders and its own aims. They launched attacks on military installations and other symbols of the government. In August 1992, for example, a bomb was set off at Algiers International Airport that killed 10 and wounded 128.

The government responded by cracking down on religious freedoms. Mosques, particularly those thought to be led by radical preachers, were no longer safe havens. Instead, worshipers found themselves praying while being watched by riot police. Muslim leaders suspected of being connected to the FIS were put under 24-hour surveillance. Their phones were tapped, and their mail was opened.[8] In December 1992, the government imposed a nighttime curfew in Algiers and in the cities of Blida, Tipaza, Boumerdès, Ain-Delfa, and Bouira.

The fighting soon intensified. Independent groups, operating in a series of small cells, began a campaign of urban violence that devastated Algeria. Government officials were assassinated. Car bombs were set off. Army barracks were attacked. Police officers were murdered. The attacks were happening daily; the government barely recovered from one before the next occurred. In March 1994, terrorists stopped a passenger train. The 300 passengers were ordered to get off the train, and the carriages were then set on fire. In September, more than 500 schools were set afire.

Vigilante groups began to roam the streets, terrifying the people into accepting their new social laws. Residents in Blida, for example, were forced to remove satellite dishes that broadcast Western films, and women were prohibited from seeing male doctors. Shops selling alcohol and videos were forced to close down. By joining these terrorist cells, young men who had been unemployed and powerless now found themselves able to dictate terms to terrified citizens. Soon, their demands grew more and more outrageous and the violence more extreme. The government seemed powerless to restore order.

The campaign of terror also targeted teachers, professors, writers, journalists, and lawyers. Many received death threats or worse. Omar Belhouchet, the editor of a daily newspaper in Algiers, dropped his children off at school one day in May 1994. Checking to be sure that they had safely entered the school, he suddenly spotted two gunmen running toward his car and firing. Dropping down onto the front seat, he stepped on the accelerator and managed to escape.[9] He chose to stay in Algeria, although he sent his children to stay with relatives in France. Hundreds of other journalists fled in the mayhem.

The violence continued, month after month. Groups such as the Groupes Islamiques Armés (GIA)—Islamic Armed Group—and the Mouvement Islamique Armé (MIA)—Islamic Armed Movement—were among those claiming responsibility for the attacks. The government responded with increasing violence of its own; reportedly, government-sponsored paramilitary groups carried out revenge killings and mass arrests. The violence even spread to foreign targets. In July 1995, the GIA exploded a bomb on the Paris subway system; in December, members of the group hijacked an Air France airliner in Algeria. In all, nearly 100,000 people were killed in 10 years of terrorist attacks and violent reprisals.

ALGERIA TODAY

Unlike the war with France that ended in 1962, there is no specific date when the civil war that marked Algeria in the 1990s ended. Violence and killings continue sporadically, although most of the main terrorist groups had been defeated or accepted the government's offer of amnesty by 2002. In April 1999, the military's candidate, Abdelaziz Bouteflika, won elections that were boycotted by Islamist parties.

Bouteflika had a reputation as a pro-Western liberal. His initial strategy focused on determining how best to appeal to the young Algerians who had been attracted to extremist groups because of the lack of other opportunities. He sought to revitalize the economy and restore Algerians' pride in their country. He also focused on bringing an end to the violence and civil war by addressing the factors that had caused it to spring up in the first place.

In order to bring the warring factions together, Bouteflika proposed what amounted to an amnesty for the terrorist groups. They could return to society without ever facing charges for the violence that they had enacted upon the population. Those who had suffered, and the families of those killed, were angered by this apparent pardon of murderers. These families claimed that the killers were escaping simply because the government wanted to hold onto power.

That anger still simmers beneath the surface in Algeria. Years of war and high unemployment continue to hamper economic recovery. Oil revenues have helped, but most ordinary Algerians do not benefit from their country's oil wealth. The government had attempted to address unrest among Algeria's young people by encouraging them to open small businesses

Abdelaziz Bouteflika is the current president of Algeria, serving in the capacity since 1999. His presidency has been marked by challenges; in 2010 and 2011, he resisted street protests calling for his resignation.

such as cybercafés and restaurants. There are few barriers to emigration, and many Algerians leave to find work in foreign countries, most often France.

Peace in Algeria remains fragile and is frequently threatened. In April 2007, a series of coordinated bomb attacks rocked Algiers, killing 33 and wounding 222. The office of the prime minister was targeted in these attacks, as was a police station in the outskirts of the city. A group affiliated with Al-Qaeda in Algeria claimed responsibility for the attacks. Other attacks included a December 2006 attack on a bus carrying workers for the U.S. company Halliburton, and bombings in April, July, and September 2007—all linked to Al-Qaeda.

Human rights abuses are another concern, particularly in light of the fact that the government's rigid control makes it difficult for international monitors to verify claims of torture and other abuses. Bouteflika's hold on power also has prompted criticism. The promise once raised of multiparty elections and democratic choices has proved short-lived. Bouteflika was reelected president for a third term in April 2009.

In 1962, having achieved its independence from France after more than 130 years of colonialism, Algeria was considered to be a leader in the Third World, a symbol of the determination of a conquered people to achieve their freedom. But the hope that heralded the start of independence did not last long. The leaders who had encouraged the people to free themselves from an oppressive regime too often proved to be corrupt and willing to take extreme measures to cement their hold on power. The economy has never fully recovered from the departure of the French, despite the discovery of oil and gas reserves.

In the country's early history, Algerians were not a single people, nor was Algeria a defined territory. The borders of Algeria were formed by conquest, and its people were most clearly unified in the struggle to achieve their independence. But modern Algeria still bears certain striking resemblances to the Algeria before independence. Most of its people are excluded from positions of power and cannot lobby for demo-cratic change. They are struggling with poverty and have been robbed of certain basic rights. They want the opportunity to find meaningful work and protection from violence. It is clear that while Algeria achieved its independence five decades ago, the struggle for freedom continues.

CHRONOLOGY

1827   Dispute between French and Ottoman diplomats sparks conflict; French ships form blockade around Algiers.

1830   French troops begin landing on Algerian soil on June 14. Algiers surrenders on July 5.

1834   France formally annexes occupied territory of Algeria under the name "French possessions in the north of Africa."

1847   French military establishes control over most of Algeria; Marshal Bugeaud is named Algeria's governor-general.

1881   Northern Algeria is formally divided into three French departments; Code de l'Indigénat is passed, placing greater restrictions on Algeria's Muslim population.

1930   Celebrations to mark a century of French rule in Algeria trigger unrest.

1936   Blum-Viollette bill to pave the way for French citizenship for some Algerians is introduced, triggering violent protests from colons; bill is never passed.

1942   American forces land in North Africa and liberate Algeria during World War II.

1945   Protests in Sétif trigger violence and murder.

1954   Revolutionary Committee for Unity and Action is formed with the goal of preparing the country for an armed struggle for independence; later is reorganized into the FLN; attacks on November 1 mark the beginning of the war for independence.

1957   FLN carries out more than 800 attacks in the spring.

1958   Committee of Safety is formed by colons on May 13, and attacks on French government offices follow; Charles de Gaulle becomes leader of France; FLN announces formation of provisional government.

1959   De Gaulle offers Algerians the promise of self-determination once peace is restored; colons form Front National Français.

1962   Document recognizing Algerian independence is signed on March 18; Algerians vote for independence on July 1; Ahmed Ben Bella becomes first elected president in September.

1965   Algerian army seizes power in military coup on June 19.

TIMELINE

1827
Dispute between French and Ottoman diplomats sparks conflict; French ships form blockade around Algiers.

1936
Blum-Viollette bill to pave the way for French citizenship to some Algerians is introduced, triggering violent protests from colons; bill is never passed.

1827

1954

1954

1830
French troops begin landing on Algerian soil on June 14. Algiers surrenders on July 5.

1847
French military establishes control over most of Algeria; Marshal Bugeaud is named Algeria's governor-general.

1969   Algeria joins OPEC.

1978   Chadli Bendjedid becomes president.

1988   Riots rock Algiers on October 5, leading to "Black October" crisis.

1992   Islamic militants launch civil war; violence continues for nearly a decade.

1999   Abdelaziz Bouteflika is elected president.

2006-2007   Terrorist attacks in Algiers are linked to a group affiliated with Al-Qaeda.

2009   Bouteflika is reelected president for a third term.

1958
Committee of Safety is formed by colons on May 13, and attacks on French government offices follow.

1962
Document recognizing Algerian independence is signed on March 18; Algerians vote for independence on July 1; Ahmed Ben Bella becomes first elected president in September.

1958

1992

1959
De Gaulle offers Algerians the promise of self-determination once peace is restored; colons form Front National Français.

1965
Algerian army seizes power in military coup on June 19.

1992
Islamic militants launch civil war; violence continues for nearly a decade.

1988
Riots rock Algiers on October 5, leading to "Black October" crisis.

NOTES

CHAPTER 1

1. Edgar O'Ballance, *The Algerian Insurrection, 1954–62.* Hamden, Conn.: Archon Books, 1967, p. 22.
2. Quoted in Alistair Horne, *A Savage War of Peace: Algeria 1954–1962.* New York: Penguin Books, 1987, p. 37.
3. Ibid.
4. David Macey, *Frantz Fanon: A Biography.* New York: Picador, 2000, p. 97.
5. O'Ballance, *The Algerian Insurrection, 1954–62*, p. 33.
6. Horne, *A Savage War of Peace: Algeria 1954–1962*, p. 27.

CHAPTER 2

1. John B. Wolf, *The Barbary Coast: Algeria under the Turks.* New York: W.W. Norton, 1979, p. 6.
2. Ibid., p. 8.
3. Ibid., p. 10.

CHAPTER 3

1. John Ruedy, *Modern Algeria: The Origins and Development of a Nation.* Bloomington: Indiana University Press, 1992, p. 46.
2. Michael K. Clark, *Algeria in Turmoil: A History of the Rebellion.* New York: Frederick A. Praeger, 1959, p. 16.
3. Ruedy, *Modern Algeria*, p. 47.
4. Ibid., p. 48.
5. Ibid.
6. Ibid.

7. Quoted in Ibid., p. 50.
8. Clark, *Algeria in Turmoil*, p. 16.
9. Anthony Ham, Nana Luckham, and Anthony Sattin, *Algeria.* Oakland, Calif.: Lonely Planet, 2007, p. 30.
10. Quoted in Martin Evans and John Phillips, *Algeria: Anger of the Dispossessed.* New Haven, Conn.: Yale University Press, 2007, p. 29.

CHAPTER 4

1. Evans and Phillips, *Algeria: Anger of the Dispossessed*, p. 30.
2. Ibid., p. 31.
3. Ibid., p. 33.
4. Ibid., p. 34.
5. Ruedy, *Modern Algeria*, p. 91.
6. Evans and Phillips, *Algeria: Anger of the Dispossessed*, p. 38.
7. Ruedy, *Modern Algeria*, p. 121.
8. Evans and Phillips, *Algeria: Anger of the Dispossessed*, p. 39.

CHAPTER 5

1. Horne, *A Savage War of Peace: Algeria 1954–1962*, p. 36.
2. Quoted in Ibid.
3. Quoted in Ibid., p. 37.
4. Quoted in Ibid.
5. Quoted in Ibid., p. 40.
6. Clark, *Algeria in Turmoil*, p. 21.
7. Quoted in Ibid., pp. 22–23.

CHAPTER 6

1. Horne, *A Savage War of Peace: Algeria 1954–1962*, p. 43.

2. Quoted in Evans and Phillips, *Algeria: Anger of the Dispossessed*, p. 52.

3. Ibid., p. 55.

4. Ibid., p. 57.

5. Ibid.

CHAPTER 7

1. Quoted in Horne, *A Savage War of Peace: Algeria 1954–1962*, p. 99.

2. Quoted in Ibid., p. 101.

3. Ruedy, *Modern Algeria*, pp. 172–173.

4. Ibid., p. 173.

CHAPTER 8

1. Evans and Phillips, *Algeria: Anger of the Dispossessed*, p. 67.

2. Ibid., p. 69.

3. Ibid., p. 70.

4. Ruedy, *Modern Algeria*, p. 186.

5. Ibid, p. 192.

6. Ham, Luckham, and Sattin, *Algeria*, p. 34.

CHAPTER 9

1. Ruedy, *Modern Algeria*, p. 195.

2. Quoted in Horne, *A Savage War of Peace: Algeria 1954–1962*, p. 540.

3. Quoted in Ruedy, *Modern Algeria*, p. 207.

4. Quoted in Evans and Phillips, *Algeria: Anger of the Dispossessed*, p. 84.

5. Ibid., p. 87.

6. Ibid., p. 104.

7. Quoted in Ibid., p. 161.

8. Ibid., p. 185.

9. Ibid., p. 191.

BIBLIOGRAPHY

BOOKS

Clark, Michael K. *Algeria in Turmoil: A History of the Rebellion*. New York: Frederick A. Praeger, 1959.

Evans, Martin, and John Phillips. *Algeria: Anger of the Dispossessed*. New Haven, Conn.: Yale University Press, 2007.

Fanon, Frantz (trans. by Richard Philcox). *The Wretched of the Earth*. New York: Grove Press, 2004.

Galula, David. *Pacification in Algeria: 1956–1958*. Santa Monica, Calif.: RAND, 2006.

Gordon, David C. *The Passing of French Algeria*. New York: Oxford University Press, 1966.

Ham, Anthony, Nana Luckham, and Anthony Sattin. *Algeria*. Oakland, Calif.: Lonely Planet, 2007.

Horne, Alistair. *A Savage War of Peace: Algeria 1954–1962*. New York: Penguin, 1987.

Macey, David. *Frantz Fanon: A Biography*. New York: Picador, 2000.

O'Ballance, Edgar. *The Algerian Insurrection, 1954–62*. Hamden, Conn.: Archon Books, 1967.

Porch, Douglas. *The Conquest of the Sahara*. New York: Alfred A. Knopf, 1984.

Ruedy, John. *Modern Algeria: The Origins and Development of a Nation*. Bloomington: Indiana University Press, 1992.

Wilkin, Anthony. *Among the Berbers of Algeria*. New York: Cassell & Company, 1900.

Wolf, John B. *The Barbary Coast: Algeria Under the Turks*. New York: W.W. Norton, 1979.

WEB SITES

"Algeria," *New York Times*. Available online. URL: http://topics
.nytimes.com/top/news/international/countriesandterritories/
algeria/index.html?scp=1-spot&sq=Algeria&st=cse.

"Algeria Country Profile," BBC. Available online. URL: http://
news.bbc.co.uk/2/hi/africa/country_profiles/790556.stm.

Dirksen, Everett M. "May 8, In Paris on VE Day." The Dirksen
Congressional Center. Available online. URL: http://www.
dirksencenter.org/1945trip/may8text.htm.

Gawalt, Gerard W. "America and the Barbary Pirates: An
International Battle against an Unconventional Foe." The
Library of Congress. Available online. URL: http://memory.
loc.gov/ammem/collections/jefferson_papers/mtjprece.html.

Gjersø, J.F. "La Guerre d'Algérie." The Civilising Mission.
Available online. URL: http://thecivilisingmission.com/2010/
06/09/la-guerre-d-algerie/.

Jefferson, Thomas. "Autobiography," Liberty Online. Available
online. URL: http://libertyonline.hypermall.com/Jefferson/
Autobiography.html.

Permanent Mission of Algeria to the United Nations. Available
online. URL: http://www.algeria-un.org.

"World War 2 History," World War 2. Available online.
URL: http://www.world-war-2.info/history/.

FURTHER RESOURCES

BOOKS

DiPiazza, Francesca Davis. *Algeria in Pictures*. Minneapolis, Minn.: Lerner Publishing, 2008.

Kagda, Falaq, and Zawiah Abdul Latif. *Algeria*. New York: Marshall Cavendish, 1997.

Morgan, Ted. *My Battle of Algiers*. New York: Smithsonian Books, 2005.

Rogerson, Barnaby. *A Traveller's History of North Africa*, 2nd ed. Northampton, Mass.: Interlink Publishing, 2000.

Stora, Benjamin. *Algeria, 1830–2000: A Short History*. Ithaca, N.Y.: Cornell University Press, 2001.

WEB SITES

Algeria Daily News Site
http://algeriadaily.com/

BBC News Algeria Country Profile
http://news.bbc.co.uk/2/hi/africa/country_profiles/790556.stm

CIA World Factbook Report on Algeria
https://www.cia.gov/library/publications/the-world-factbook/geos/ag.html

Embassy of Algeria to the United States
http://www.algeria-us.org/

Norwegian Council for Africa
http://afrika.no/English/index.html

PICTURE CREDITS

INDEX

ABOUT THE AUTHOR

HEATHER LEHR WAGNER is a writer and editor. She is the author of more than 50 books that explore political and social issues for middle school and high school readers. She earned a B.A. in political science from Duke University and an M.A. in government from the College of William and Mary.